Ask God
for a
MIRACLE

Also by Ginger Mostert Church:
A Woman's Walk With God

Ask God *for a* MIRACLE

Your Life Will Never Be the Same

GINGER MOSTERT CHURCH

REVIEW AND HERALD® PUBLISHING ASSOCIATION
HAGERSTOWN, MD 21740

This book was
Edited by Patricia Fritz
Copyedited by James Cavil
Cover designed by Freshcut Design
Cover photos by PictureQuest
Interior design by Candy Harvey
Electronic makeup by Shirley M. Bolivar
Typeset: 12.5/15 Bembo

PRINTED IN U.S.A.
05 04 03 02 01   5 4 3 2 1

R&H Cataloging Service
Church, Ginger Mostert, 1945-   .
    Ask God for a miracle.

        1. Spiritual life.   I. Title.

            248

ISBN 0-8280-1898-7

Dedicated to my two wonderful
daughters-in-law, Melody and Michelle,
who have added
so much joy to my life and
taught me
so many things.

To my four siblings,
Tom, Kathy, Patty, and Betty;
they are truly
examples and encouragers to me.

And to the memory of my parents,
Thomas and Hildreth Mostert,
both asleep in Jesus
awaiting His glorious return.

·⌣ Contents ⌣·

"WHAT WOULD YOU HAVE ME DO, LORD?"

Have you ever tried to run away from God? No, I don't mean like Jonah, who boarded a ship and deliberately sailed toward an unknown destination. Not even like the prodigal son, who took all his earthly goods and wasted them on frivolous living.

The running described in these pages tells of an ordinary young woman groping through life with dulled vision. Her direction clouded, she settled for less than God's plan for her. The "joy of the Lord" that she longed for often turned to sorrow and despair. Lonely days affected her life, as well as those of her husband and two sons, whom she loved dearly. Focusing too often on *Gotta get through another day,* she almost buried her zest for real living. *Why am I so lonely?* The words echoed repeatedly inside her unchallenged mind.

Perhaps you will find yourself here. You might be a runaway: lonely, discouraged, and ready to give up. You might be a son or a daughter who has seen better, yet has settled for unacceptable. Could it be that you've been seeing yourself through human eyes, rather than through God's eyes? as a failure, rather than an intrinsic part of God's perfect plan?

Open your heart. Catch the excitement of His blueprint for your life. As you accept yourself as God's agent, a person whom God saw clearly in the womb, you'll want to be still, study often, and know that you are approved and living daily in the way God's children are destined to live.

Often I asked God to let me forget this story. To help me remember only the good times—the happy times—in my life. Why would I want to share all the "loser" parts of an ordinary life?

Yet, if by telling my story one person realizes that God has made each of His children in His image—perfect—it will be worth the effort. Life is precious and short. I want to share with others so that they have more time to flourish and grow and develop for God.

Once I mentioned to God that I'd told my story enough. "I'm not telling it anymore," I said as I talked and walked with Him. "It makes me look too bad. Thank You for understanding and not requiring that of me."

God remained silent. A week went by; two, three, and more. I had been asked to present a worship talk to a group of about 50 men and women who had come to the Review and Herald for a writers' workshop. One thing I knew: I wouldn't be telling "My Story."

God must have chuckled. He gave me time for my heart to soften. His plans were not my plans. The day that I got up to speak, one of the women raised her hand. "Ginger," she requested, "tell us your story. Many of the folks here have not heard it before."

After that, I told God that whenever He would be

glorified, I would tell my story. It's really His story of my life. I wouldn't change a thing.

Looking back over my walk with God, I see that the times that I couldn't see the light were necessary to build trust in my life and give me understanding into the hardships of others. Could I take a moment away—any moment—I would not. Truly God has had a plan for me, and I would not want to miss any part of it.

Growth stretches us. Development takes a lot of falling down and getting up. You and I, made in the image of God, came with a lot of rough edges that must be polished. It's painful work—but worth the effort when He makes us into the jewels that we were meant to be.

Where would I be if He hadn't had the patience to make me and mold me?

~· Chapter 1 ~·

FEAR—A BEAST AND A BURDEN

"Let your conduct be without covetousness; be content with such things as you have. For He Himself has said, 'I will never leave you nor forsake you' " (Hebrews 13:5).

*P*lease stop. Don't go. We need you! Unwanted tears sprang again from my eyes with new intensity as the taillights of our car disappeared from view. *I will have a whole week of "When is Daddy coming home?"* How would I make it?

Two innocent boys, turning from their waving, joined their weeping mother in her "pity party." The house seemed empty and cold without Dennis, my husband and their father. How would we occupy the endless hours until we were a family again? Yes, he had taken our only vehicle. But I had two good legs, and a small shopping complex, with everything we would need, was only a few blocks away. Yet I borrowed unknown troubles as pictures of snowy wrecks and other unknown disasters flashed before my eyes. Fear wound itself around my heart and wouldn't let go.

LORD, IS THIS WHAT YOU WANT FOR MY LIFE?
Why am I alone, afraid, and unhappy? These questions

and others often troubled me. Wasn't God good? Shouldn't I trust Him? Had He ever let me down?

As an answer to one of those questions, my grief overflowed and my thoughts wandered momentarily to the recent loss of my father. He had been my rock, my hero. He wrote often and encouraged me as only a beloved parent can. Now he was gone, taken suddenly by a final illness at only age 55. Life wasn't fair. *God, I can't seem to find the key to happiness. Are You here? How could I live through another loss? How can I find joy again?*

That day, as I'd done so often before, I dried my tears and sent Doug and Dony off to play. Alone with my thoughts, my mind wandered to Dennis and our courting days. We'd begun dating our senior year at Ozark Academy in Gentry, Arkansas. Dennis reminded me of so many of the good qualities in my father. He worked hard, he enjoyed eating (even eating out, which made me—a collector of "I can't cook" jokes—very happy), and his happy, even-tempered personality put an extra spark into my life.

After our graduation Dennis returned home to Loma Linda, California, and I went back to my home in Shreveport, Louisiana. Seven months passed before I would see him again, for a wonderful Christmas holiday.

We enjoyed 10 glorious days of getting reacquainted, catching up on all that we'd missed while apart. We joined his friends for laughter and adventure. A trip to the Tournament of Roses parade made the holiday extra-special but almost wore us out. Leaving California and my love nearly broke my heart.

A few months later a miracle seemed to happen when my father accepted a call to be a pastor in central California. In the spring, with my family gone, Keene, Texas, where I was attending college, seemed deserted. What joy when, during spring break, Dennis and a couple of his friends made the quick trip to Keene and helped me transfer to La Sierra College in southern California!

During the next couple of years Dennis and I talked about marriage and the home we would build together. We each shared the things that were important to us.

We both wanted two children. Dennis, in his no-nonsense way, had two *important* requests. Number one: "I don't do dishes," he laughed softly. "I did enough as a child, and I just don't ever want to do any more." That seemed reasonable to me. I liked to do dishes. And besides, we'd eat out a lot, I was sure. Number two: "I don't change baby diapers!" At the time I couldn't see that this would be a problem.

As I think back, it's an especially good thing that we'd both agreed on his second request. With Dennis's very healthy gag reflex, all sorts of things made him choke. Dirty diapers and throwing-up kids made him walk fast in any direction, lest he add to the mess.

I'd made only one request to Dennis: "I don't want to be left alone at night. I like people around, and I like someone to talk to. As long as you come home right after work, I'll be great!"

Where had we gone wrong? During the past few years I'd find myself tearful during the days before an upcoming trip. No matter how hard I'd try to tell myself, *You will do better the next time—Dennis has to be gone just a day or two,* I couldn't shake the beast of fear and the burden of loneliness that held me captive.

Together we'd made the decision to move to Omaha, Nebraska. He'd been offered a position at a branch of Pacific Press Publishing Association. Knowing that this job required some traveling, Dennis had already turned it down once. The second time the call came, we both knew that this must be God's will for us; and, as a family, we picked up and moved.

But, I'm getting ahead of myself. The real story began years before. It goes back to the beginning of the fear. It begins with the "beast and the burden" that continually haunted me and made me angry and sad.

Chapter 2

"If Only . . . ; But I Can't"

"Train up a child in the way he should go, and when he is old he will not depart from it" (Proverbs 22:6).

O r will he? If you are a parent or considering children in your future, ask yourself this question: "What does it take to raise a child successfully?" Would you say it takes godly parents to "train up a child in the way he should go"? Yes, godly parents are the ideal. The offspring they produce definitely have a head start.

While a host of mighty workers have come from Christ-centered families, history tells us of many giants for God who came from backgrounds that would make us shudder. Even today, examples such as the outstanding Christian pediatric neurosurgeon Dr. Ben Carson and the U.S. Senate chaplain Rear Admiral Barry C. Black came from single-parent homes in which daily life proved hard and lonely for parent and child.

Other great leaders, such as Ron Halvorsen, came from gangs. God found Jack Blanco despite his atheistic background. Others have had learning disabilities, such as dyslexia. Some have come from families in which Christ was ignored, His name either forbidden or blasphemed.

The fact remains: we can find dedicated Christian workers who were raised in atmospheres in which the name of Jesus has never been heard and certainly never spoken. You and I worship and minister alongside men and women who turned to God and gave Him their lives despite the threat of death or disownment. Their sacrifice to follow God cannot be imagined or understood by most Christians today.

The common ingredient in a life dedicated to God can always be traced back to God's call, to the wooing of the Holy Spirit and an answer of "Yes, Lord, I trust You with my life. You take this fragile, sinful body and make it over into a vessel fit for Your service."

Praise God for dedicated, loving parents! But don't despair if your heritage is less than ideal. When God looks for servants, He finds the most willing. The most useful and even the best often come from the least capable. *"But God has chosen the foolish things of the world to put to shame the wise, and God has chosen the weak things of the world to put to shame the things which are mighty"* *(1 Corinthians 1:27)*. *"And He said to me, 'My grace is sufficient for you, for My strength is made perfect in weakness.' Therefore most gladly I will rather boast in my infirmities, that the power of Christ may rest upon me. Therefore I take pleasure in infirmities, in reproaches, in needs, in persecutions, in distresses, for Christ's sake. For when I am weak, then I am strong"* *(2 Corinthians 12:9, 10).*

God has a plan for every one of His children. None can say, "I just wasn't good enough, smart enough, or even wise enough." As humans we choose the best. We look for the man or woman most endowed with personal talents. God looks for a willing heart.

I found myself stumped and totally hung up when I came face to face with another life-changing question: How do I recognize if I am in God's will?

The answer belongs to God alone. We will begin to understand the answer when we talk to Jesus face to face. Sin happens. Lucifer, that glorious angel in the heavenly courts, became jealous. He made bad choices. The beauty of God's love is that we get to choose. We are His children. We grow by making right choices and through exercising our will.

Yes, the choices are ours. We can choose life or death, service or selfishness, sin or salvation. Humans look for a formula. God looks at the heart—the willingness. We see others an hour, a day, a few years. God sees our whole life.

Are we left to worry and wonder? Is there a set of instructions that we should follow? Before we answer these questions, I need to take you back in my story.

THE STORY OF A LOSER

From my first recollections of life, serving others always seemed to be at the top of my parents' list of priorities for my brother, three sisters, and me. We were raised for service. We had a direction, a calling. From childhood we knew that God loved us. We were dedicated to Him as babies. As youngsters we were taught that no sacrifice would be too great when it came to following God. How often I've heard it said, "God is a hard master!" Yet in our family, being a child of God truly brought joy and gave us a multitude of happy memories.

As children we practiced soul winning through the daily chore of dishwashing. We didn't just rinse the dishes—we baptized them! Traveling to a second church on Sabbath with our pastor father, we would often take sides of the highway and count the wires on all telephone poles within eyesight. The number of wires on the pole meant the number of converts each evangelistic team had.

Our favorite times were spent singing. What joy praises to God brought to our hearts! The way we chose our songs made it really special. Instead of someone saying, "What will we sing next?" our singing just flowed from one song to another. Someone, usually our father from the driver's seat, began the singing with something like "Do, Lord." Mother and all of us kids would quickly join in and attempt to find harmonizing parts. We would continue singing as many verses as possible.

The end of that first song would bring the BIG challenge: Who would be first to start the next song? Our family had an unwritten rule that we all knew and loved: The next song had to have a word from the previous song's title or first line in its title or first line. Thus after "Do, Lord" could come "Lord, in the Morning," followed by "In the morning I see His face," and then "Face to Face" or "I Shall See the King." How quickly the miles sailed by and our love for Jesus grew.

Somehow, before we reached home, our favorite

song would always be sung: "Were You There?" First the verse ". . . crucified my Lord," then ". . . nailed Him to the tree." We could feel the darkness during ". . . the sun refused to shine," and feel the silence after ". . . they laid Him in the tomb." The glorious moment came when we lifted our voices and sang out, "Were you there when He rose up from the dead?" Finally we finished with ". . . when He comes to take us home."

Often "I'm Homesick for Heaven" followed. Usually we would end with "We Are Climbing Jacob's Ladder" or "Lord, Build Me a Cabin in the Corner of Glory Land," a wonderful Southern gospel song.

The messages wrapped in these songs and many others gave each of us a strong foundation. The stories that they conveyed served as a rock or foundation for each of us to build on. Oh yes, we were placed on this earth to bless others! So why do I share this sad story? Could a loser come from such a positive, Christ-centered home?

The years passed. Serve we did. Sometimes we got involved in passing out literature. We sang at the funerals of strangers whom we would never know. Some weeks found us helping in children's divisions. We were doing our best with the talents we had.

I did serve until my teen years. Those are the hard years that each person must live through, when boys and girls turn into men and women. Each young person looks inward, and then at others around them, and begins to make a judgment call. *I am not worthy! What can I possibly do? Everyone has more talent.* Or: *I am just not good enough. It's time for me to take a break.* Or: *Why didn't they pick me? I'm losing it.* You get the picture. *Of course I'd be involved if I were the best. They really don't need me when so many others can do a better job. Let me rest for a season. Oh no! I've lost it! Better to sit it out than to make a fool of myself.* "If only . . . ; but I can't" became my new focus.

I'll stop here. Unless I'm mistaken, you've said some of these very things yourself. You've felt that pressure of never being good enough. Perhaps you, too, almost gave up on yourself. What a burden to bear! What a messed-up picture I had of myself and of God! Yet more and more I became less involved with blessing others and using the abilities that God had built into that speck in my mother's womb.

Chapter 3

"I Do" and
"I Don't Want to"

*"Now the Lord came and stood and called as at other times,
'Samuel! Samuel!' And Samuel answered, 'Speak, for Your
servant hears'" (1 Samuel 3:10, 11).*

We married during the Vietnam War years. War
has a way of increasing the intensity of one's life,
and indeed it did with ours. How often I had thought
about this marriage adventure. You know: *I'll be the perfect wife. At first it'll be just the two of us, and then two children. We'll never have a dull moment; nor will we want for
anything.* Yet taking these dreams and turning them into
reality soon began stretching us and taking us outside
our comfort zone.

At first, moving from one apartment to another
added spice to our married life. Dennis continued attending college, and I found a job. Less than a year later
we discovered a real taste of the hardships of life: the
dentist's office where I worked decided to downsize, and
I found myself out of a job and three months pregnant.

What a time! I look back now and call it growth.
We were getting experience in the nitty-gritty of life; it
was one of the first bumps we would face in our mar-

riage. Hard times stretched our faith. I found another position; I could even walk to work. Dennis thinks back and, at times, laments the fact that he spent many of his wonderful old collectible coins to put food on the table and gas in the car.

We marvel how, because of the host of single young men in southern California, a miracle pregnancy, and Dennis's surprise reclassification just before he was to be drafted for a tour of duty in Vietnam, we were not separated at that time. Life was good! Surely God loved us and wanted only the best for us.

Life rocked on for a time after that. We moved into a little rental house. I became a stay-at-home mother. What else could we need?

God knew. Dennis's college roommate and best man in our wedding, Russ Potter, encouraged us to apply for a job at the Pacific Press Publishing Association, where he so enjoyed working. He told us about the opportunities there, which got us excited. I enjoyed the friendship of his wife, Sheryl, and we knew it would be fun being together again. Hadn't we enjoyed being next-door neighbors during the first six months of our marriage? We checked out the place, but it just didn't seem to fit our needs—so we forgot about moving and starting over.

God didn't! The call to join the staff of Pacific Press in Mountain View, California, came one sunny afternoon. Dennis loved books. Yet since the job he was being offered didn't seem right for us, he again was forced to answer, "We're not interested!"

They didn't want to take his no for an answer.

A NEW CHAPTER

We packed up and rented a U-Haul trailer. Despite the fact that I was once again pregnant, we found ourselves moving to Mountain View, California. Another adventure. Could this be the best one yet? It didn't take long for that question to be answered.

With the birth of our second son, Dony, and the need to move into a two-bedroom place, we found ourselves struggling. The pay that Dennis received just didn't cover our expenses in this high-priced area. Soon our free evenings were replaced with Dennis's long hours of overtime. Then he took a second job—a part-time night job.

Part of the dream Dennis and I cherished included my being a stay-at-home mom to our children, and we just couldn't give that up. Yet hard questions nagged us. *Were we to give up on the part of our life plan in which Dennis would be home all night? How long could he keep up this hectic pace?*

Things seemed to turn around when we found a perfect little house within bike-riding distance of Dennis's work. We moved in less than three months after Dony's birth—our third move that year. Life was good. What more could I ask? I now had a washer and a dryer, instead of making multiple trips to the Laundromat. Finally we had a fenced yard with shade trees in the back.

"DON'T GET TOO COMFORTABLE"

Comfort is a relative term. We can be comfortable with much or with little. Often that happens in the mind. We felt content and in control of our lives. What a great feeling!

Then, out of the blue, Dennis got a message to "report to the boss's office immediately."

What could they want now? He wondered as he headed in that direction.

Dennis called and told me about it a bit later on that warm sunny day.

"Management wants us to move to Omaha, Nebraska," he began. "They say it will be a move up the company ladder. I told them an emphatic 'No!' I think they got the point."

He went on to say that they had asked him three things: (1) Do you like to travel? (2) Do you like to preach? (3) Do you want to move? Since all three seemed out of the question to him, there seemed to be no need to pursue the conversation.

What a relief I felt! Most of our family lived in California. We needed to stay in California. Why would we want to leave California? The weather—who could beat the close-to-perfect weather we enjoyed year-round in Mountain View? The final straw would be to move again. No, I agreed with Dennis. It would be in our best interest to "stay put."

WHEN NO ISN'T THE RIGHT ANSWER

Two wonderful weeks passed. Eight months in the same place—I could get used to this. Our moving days were over.

God doesn't give up. Were we too comfortable? In

eternity we will see the whole picture. A few days later Dennis once again found himself making his way to the boss's office. He wondered about God's persistence. The gist of their one-sided conversation went like this:

"We know you aren't interested in moving. You made that quite plain. Yet we feel the job that is available in Omaha, Nebraska, has just the right components for you. It will be a great career move. Think of it this way: 'When the train comes into the station, you better get on. Who knows when the right train will come again?'"

Dennis's call shattered my morning. "Honey, they need me. They need us to move. I know it will be hard . . ." I heard no more. I could not speak. My bravery had dissolved into tears.

Footsteps on the porch let me know that my wonderful man had come home to be with me, to comfort me. So we could plan and pray together. Despite our desperate desire to "stay put," we both felt that "when God called" we must answer "Yes" to His will.

Since the beginning of time, children have left their parents and traveled to places unknown. Yet, as the days went by, we began to seriously question our decision. In the flurry of activity we almost forgot that each new journey brings new circumstances and different hurdles to jump.

I tried to stay strong. Where had that we-can-do-anything girl gone?

The next weeks were a whirlwind of packing, of saying goodbye to our family and friends. We had little money, still very little of this world's goods; Omaha seemed like the other side of the earth. Tears came often as I felt helpless and hopeless. In his new position Dennis would be traveling a lot. I would be alone.

"Why did You pick us, God? I love Dennis, but please, I don't want to move to the middle of nowhere. Omaha, Nebraska, seems to be a cowboy town of stockyards and, I fear, even dirt roads. Is this where You want us to raise our boys?"

My imagination played havoc with my mind. Unhappiness nipped at my heels and weighed me down. During the drive across the country our baby, Dony, became sick and gave us quite a scare. With each passing day our lovely adventure turned slowly into an unending nightmare.

"Don't borrow trouble. Live today and let tomorrow take care of itself."

How, Lord? Are You even with us? We seem so alone.

We got there three days before the moving truck was due, only to learn that it had arrived before us. We had no place to live, and we also had an impatient driver wanting to unload our furniture.

"There's a rental you can temporarily move into," we were told when Dennis called his boss back in California. "You can live there until you find something else."

What a house! A mess I didn't want to face. "Dirty" doesn't describe what I saw and felt that day. I didn't want a purple bedroom. Awnings covered the windows and blocked the sun. *And what will we do about those basement stairs that the baby can fall down?*

"I want to go home. Do I have to live here?" escaped my trembling lips "Surely God made a mistake in wanting us to move here."

More tears fell. I asked "Why?" dozens of times. My poor husband couldn't answer any of them. Our faith took a beating. What else could go wrong?

"Be strong and of good courage, for you must go with this people to the land which the Lord has sworn to their fathers to give them, and you shall cause them to inherit it. And the Lord, He is the One who goes before you. He will be with you. He will not leave you nor forsake you; do not fear nor be dismayed" (Deuteronomy 31:7, 8).

As dusk settled in, we finally unloaded the last piece of furniture, brought in the last box, and sighed with relief as the truck pulled away. *We're so alone.* That unspoken feeling haunted both Dennis and me. We were alone in a house we didn't like, in a city we couldn't imagine living in, wondering what would happen next. Perhaps morning would make better sense of our circumstances.

We both fell silent. No words, it seemed, could help us now. *Had Elijah felt this lonely when he fled from Jezebel?*

Dennis finally broke the silence. "We need to call our folks and tell them we're moved in. I think we can find a phone booth at that shopping center down the road a few blocks."

We loaded the tired boys into the car. We drove down the hill, around the corner, another, and just one more.

A few minutes later after calling our parents, it became darker, and we felt the need to hurry back to our place—despite the turmoil it was in. In one swift motion Dennis put the car in gear and pressed the gas pedal.

If only he had noticed the cement parking-stall barricade in front of our wheels. Too late! The impact created the awful screech of a broken engine. How could we add yet another thing to our woes?

"I'm so lonely"

In times of deepest despair God does His mightiest work. By now most of the stores were closed. Dennis walked over to the gas station on the corner, expecting that we were doomed. On top of everything else, now we had an impossibly broken engine. We couldn't afford this setback.

In the bustle of a small but brightly lit office a man listened to Dennis's tale of woe. The stranger stroked his chin and smiled. "You know, our mechanic lives only a few blocks away. I'll give him a call. He'll be here in just a few minutes."

A moment seems like a lifetime

What do angels look like? Will we know ours when we see them?

We didn't wait long; although, with two weary children, the waiting seemed like a lifetime.

"Go ahead and open the hood, sir," the stranger directed, after he had listened to the racket while the engine ran. "You've only bent the pan. You won't hurt anything to drive it on over to the station. We'll have you on your way in no time."

Sweet words. Golden words. Words of deliverance and promise. No price would be too high. We'd figure out how to pay it somehow. Right now, just to be able to drive home . . .

If I live to be 100, I'll never forget what happened next. Five minutes or less and the hood was closed and he laughed as he said, "Your engine should be as good as new."

"What do we owe you?" Dennis asked, hoping for the best but expecting the worst, since the mechanic had had to come there from home.

"No payment needed. I was just glad I could help you. Have a wonderful evening."

SO QUICKLY WE FORGET

Both Dennis and I have never wavered. That never-to-be-forgotten night we saw our angel. We talked to him. Through his care God felt so close. God loved us and cared about us, all alone and discouraged in a far-away city. In the gathering darkness tensions drained as we drove quietly to our new home. God promises us that He understands our shortcomings. *"The Lord pities those who fear Him. For He knows our frame; He remembers that we are dust" (Psalm 103:13, 14).*

I tried to be brave. When things went wrong, I remembered His presence and the joy and warmth it brought. Then a few months later my father died suddenly. I reeled from the blow. Scraping together money for our airfares, the boys and I flew back to California for Dad's funeral. My cup of sorrow overflowed, then stayed, full to the top.

We returned home, and life went on as usual. Our

boys thrived and grew. The seasons came and went. I tried to get involved in church activities. Quickly I found that being a cradle roll leader only made me nervous. *Surely that wasn't my talent. If only they would invite me to be a greeter.* It turned out that the greeter jobs were only for those who had a long history as a member of the church—about 15 years. I warmed the pew and grew lonelier with the passing weeks.

Dennis flourished in his new position and enjoyed each new challenge. The tasks were varied, and workdays went fast. He hated to leave the boys and me while he traveled around eight states, but meeting and working with many people, attending meetings, working with salespeople, as well as doing accounting and shipping, kept him busy and inspired.

On the other hand, to meet the added expenses of a first grader in church school, I began to do childcare for six other children. Eight children can be daunting, especially when one of them cannot hear or speak, leaving me tired and in need of some adult company. Days often seemed long. Instead of doing "great" things, I suddenly knew that God had indeed made me junk and that I would live out my days in the background—lonely, too often unhappy, and seldom if ever making a difference in any person's life.

FINDING ANSWERS

Life might have gone on this way indefinitely. Most of the time things rocked along at an even pace. Except those times Dennis would share about an upcoming trip, laughter rang throughout our home. I did my best to be a good wife and mother.

We bought the plain, dirty house after renting it for six months. We cleaned and scrubbed it until it sparkled. Dennis built shelves and added a two-story playhouse in the basement for the boys, and we fenced the yard. We got new carpet, painted, and remodeled the kitchen. Together we gave it "our look." Our families visited and were surprised by the large modern city that was our home.

Yet always my prayer remained the same. *Lord, when are You taking us back to California?*

Looking back, life seemed full—except when Dennis left. Life just seemed to stop or slow to a crawl during the times Dennis traveled. "We'll go there when your daddy comes home," I'd respond to a request to do something fun. "I'll make something special for supper as soon as Daddy gets back." I might as well have said, "Your dad is gone on a trip—let's just put life on hold."

You'd think I'd have welcomed the stranger at my door on that sunny spring day. You'd think that I'd have invited her in and asked her to share a warm drink and a few moments of friendship. You'd think that I would have done that. But I didn't. In fact, she was the last person I wanted to see. I may have been rude.

Tall and straightforward, she came right to the point.

Yet a lot of living came before the visit of the friend I didn't want or need. A lot of crying and searching happened. You'll meet this stranger in time, but we mustn't get ahead of the story. She seemed so out of place in my life.

Chapter 4

"There Must Be More"

*"Do not sorrow, for the joy of the Lord
is your strength" (Nehemiah 8:10).*

Friends are important. Without special friends, to whom does one go with happiness, with disappointment, or when a milestone has been reached? It seems I had been so busy wishing I could be somewhere else that I had not taken the time to reach out to others—to develop special friends. Oh yes, Dennis, my husband and best friend, made life fun and interesting; but what about the week or so a month when he had to be away?

To fill the empty hours and to save money, I sewed. I made my clothes and clothes for others. The sewing machine and I became close. I enjoyed making the boys' shirts and shorts. I found pleasure in making a leisure jacket for Dennis. I cooked. It may have been reluctant and out of necessity, but I cooked. Dennis's mom sent me scraps of fabric, and what joy I found making quilts and stuffed animals; and other things, perhaps not worth mentioning, filled my time and gave me a measure of happiness.

During these years I know that God never tired of

trying to reach me with His joy—the joy of serving others. I wanted none of it. *Leave me alone, God. Can't You see I don't have what it takes to be successful as Your servant and witness?*

As a family we canoed and picnicked. We hiked and shoveled snow. We enjoyed life. In little ways I tried to get involved with the people around me and touch others. The boys and I collected $100 for the Jerry Lewis Muscular Dystrophy Telethon, and as a family we drove to the drop-off point. Yet I couldn't get beyond the idea: *God must really be disappointed with me. My little abilities are worthless compared to those of so many others.*

When had God made me God? How could I know what He wanted and needed? I didn't see. I couldn't understand. That would take time. Humans are impatient. To God a year is as a moment. He could wait.

"MAMA, WHY DO YOU FROWN ALL THE TIME?"

Doug's question caught me off guard. Days were getting longer, and the cold winter months had been replaced by sunny, almost balmy, days. I had parked the car in front of the school, and the children and I waited for the rest of the gang. I'd like to say that on this day deep thought, perhaps borrowed worries, had creased my brow. Instead, I blamed it on the sun beating down on us through the windshield.

Doug's exuberance as he crawled into the front seat should have brought a smile to my face. Perhaps he'd had a hard day. Maybe Dennis was gone, or going, and once again I'd borrowed some unknown, unnecessary worry. Doug may have just needed encouragement. Instead, he had found a frown. In fact, he must have felt that frowns were the usual afternoon fare.

"Mama, why do you frown all the time?" he murmured as I prepared to drive away.

Like a bolt of lightning his words hit my ears. What was he saying? *Surely I, a loving Christian mother, would not, could not, be found guilty of frowning all the time. Or would I?*

"Oh, Doug," I hastily responded to our older son, "I'm not frowning—the sun is just in my eyes."

But I knew. God knew. I loved being a mother, but could this be it? What about after the boys were gone? Did God expect me to do more? How could I? What did I, or He, have to work with? Wasn't I just one of those unlucky people that God had passed by? Hadn't He missed me when giving out those "great" talents of teaching, soul winning, or preaching? My life would be doomed to "very small things."

FINDING ANSWERS

"I see that they're having a special women's meeting at the church tonight." Dennis broached the subject carefully. "Why don't you go? I'll be glad to stay home with the boys. We'll have 'boys' time,' and you just go and enjoy yourself."

What could I say? Did I want to go? Perhaps, but what if I had to sit alone? Would I just go away more discouraged? Why bother?

With no preconceived notions, I sat there that Sunday evening, listening and enjoying myself. What did I take away from that evening? Two things:

1. If I treated my husband like a king, then I would be a queen. That sounded good to me. In fact, wasn't I doing that already?

2. "We often pray for our children on a regular basis, bringing their wants and needs before God. We ask Him to make them strong and smart. We plead with Him to bring success into their lives." I nodded my head. Dennis and I had dedicated our boys to God. We wanted only the best for them—He must want that too.

The speaker that night didn't stop there. She went on:

"What about your children's spouses? Do you pray daily for God to be with them? Do you ask Him to watch over their lives? How often do you petition Him to bring these special sons and daughters of His happiness, joy, and a passion for service?

"You may laugh and say to yourself, *But my children are only babies. I'll do that later.* Begin now, tonight. You know where your children are. You know the Christian home they live in. You know the care and education they will receive. What about the one they will choose to spend their life with? Are you praying for him or her today?"

I COULD DO THAT!

I'd never thought of it before. Surely our boys would get married. But that day lay years away. I'd been busy living in the here and now. Besides, surely God had already picked the perfect girls to become wives for each of them. And yet, if I felt it so important to pray for my children, perhaps it wasn't too soon to pray for these unknown girls. I'd begin this very day! Just in case.

"I'm talking to you, Ginger"

Ginger, you pray for your husband, your children, their spouses. I'm after you. Where is your joy? These thoughts and others must have been on God's heart during those years. He never let up. I felt Him pulling, tugging, and with each new day slowly drawing me into a closer walk with Him. Yet I resisted. "Please, don't hurt me, Lord. I'm so fragile. Treat me gently."

Sabbath should have been the highlight of my week. Instead I'd go to church and heap more guilt on my burdened heart. I no longer tried to get involved. I had Dennis and the boys, and that would have to be enough.

The visiting preacher didn't seem to understand that logic. His topic was "Talents."

"We've all got talents!" he said. He seemed so full of enthusiasm. His delivery made the congregation pay attention lest we be caught looking away and he call on us. "There are some of you sitting here today that are calling me a liar." It seemed his eyes were focused right on me.

He has that right. I can't believe what he is saying. I have talents? He just doesn't know. How could he know—this man so full of passion and poise? If only he could walk in my shoes for a few days. Then he would know the sorrow and despair of wanting to do something great and finding nothing to do.

To you, reading this and having a hard time believing me, I'd like to challenge you: Today, perhaps while others in your family take a nap, I encourage you to pick up the little book *Christ's Object Lessons,* written by Ellen G. White. Turn to the chapter entitled "Talents" and study it thoroughly.

The pastor wouldn't let it drop. First he went to our mind—our mental powers. We had all been given the ability to think and learn. Yes, some more than others. Yet God does not require more from us than we are given.

OK, God. I'll try harder.

"What about your speech? Do you use your voice for God? Each of has a voice to praise God, to share God, to make His glory known to others. What are you doing with yours?"

Yes, God. I have a voice, but it is untrained. I don't know how to speak for You.

"What about your influence? You and I draw men, women, and children to God in everything we do. The little ways we walk, talk, dress, look at others; all of these are a part of our sphere of influence. Are you using your influence to glorify God?"

He caught me again, God. I'm sad, and I frown. I've really tried to change, but I don't know how. If only You would move us back to California . . . Instead, I find myself living in a city miles and miles from so many of the people I love.

The speaker didn't let up that day. I wish I knew his name. I wonder what brought him to that church on that particular Sabbath. Could it be that God sent him for me? Were others in as dire need that day as I?

"The gift of time is one of God's greatest gifts to each of us. Time is a talent. We've all been given 24 hours in our days. The choice of how we choose to use them belongs to each of us. Use it well or abuse it. Be diligent or slothful, and when the day of reckoning comes, God will ask each of us how we used this excellent talent we're now being entrusted with. How will you answer?

I'm reeling. I've been living a lie of my own choosing. God, what do You want me to say? What do You want me to do?

"Consider your health. Many of you are blessed with vigor and energy. What a talent. Are you aware that the ability to walk, run, jog, smile, eat, sleep—everything to do with health—belongs to God? It's a gift He's given you, but He will require an answer as to whether you've used it well or squandered it. Will you add to this 'glow,' gained from living within the laws that God has given us in His Word, or will you go your own way, living any way that seems good in your own eyes, paying the ultimate price of an early or painful death?"

I didn't know. I should have known. You've always loved me. You aren't the problem. My heart is broken by the pain of loneliness and loss. I'm looking backward instead of forward. Don't give up on me. I want to serve You well. Show me how. Take all of me.

THE LONGEST HOUR

I felt as if I'd been slapped. Not literally, but awakened to a world I'd forgotten. Could this man be right? Again I turned my attention to his words. Surely he couldn't have much more to say.

"As I look over this congregation, I imagine the strength it represents. Strength of the heart, mind, and soul are part of the Christian's walk. We are to love God with our heart, mind, and soul; and with all of our strength. Strength of body, of character, is what God requires of us. As we use this gift, He adds to it."

From despair to guilt . . . from guilt to hope . . . from hope to wonder . . . from wonder to acceptance. I don't know how, Lord; but I'm ready to make changes in my life if You'll walk with me every step of the way.

"Check your bank accounts. Look into your wallets and purses. From the riches of a king to the mite of a widow, God uses our money to glorify Him and be a blessing to those around us. What are you doing with yours? Are you hoarding it, or being generous in the service of the Lord? What about the widow, the orphan, the beggar? Are you using this talent to lay up treasures in heaven? Will you hold on to everything you own with a 'death grip,' or open your hands and hearts to the opportunities to give of your bounties—large or small?"

These things I pondered in my heart. I pondered and wrestled with the ideas. The concepts were what I'd always been taught, yet had lost sight of. Could I let go of my fear? Did God really expect me to use each of these things to glorify Him in my daily life?

I would go home and study for myself. Surely what this man teaches is not for everyone. His ideas were too big, and my beating heart and racing mind could take no more.

Chapter 5

"How Did I Get Here?"

"Here I am, for you did call me" (1 Samuel 3:8).

My Bible lies open on the podium. Silently I look over the sea of faces before me. I see radiant smiles, furrowed brows, fearful eyes; I feel the weight of others' grief and pain. I pause, giving each person to God, to be used for His glory.

Love them through me, Lord. Just let me touch one with the joy that only You can give.

I begin to tell a story. Through the years this story has become a story I love to tell—my story. But it was not always that way. How long did I fight God's urging to "go, and make a difference"?

I've told this same story more times than I can remember; yet it still brings tears of joy to my eyes. *Why me, God? Why me? Why have You chosen me to leave home and travel to unknown places—leaving my husband at home? You know how I mourned whenever he followed Your bidding during his traveling years. Now I am the one who leaves, and he—with that special smile and those sweet words, "Have a wonderful weekend"—keeps the home fires burning.*

Who can imagine Your ways? If You had told me what would lie ahead during the past 15 years, I surely would have run like Jonah. When did I quit fighting Your will for me and begin to accept the joy You planned for me? Can You tell me, God? Can You help me understand why You chose me—Your unlikeliest daughter? Why I am doing this?

"Why not you, My child? I promised to bless you, didn't I? Did you think I'd go back on My promises? You can trust Me. You can always trust Me."

WHEN GOD REACHES OUT

When God reaches out to a sincere child, the results cannot be told in one book. In fact, the story never ends on this earth. Each page, every story, represents an altar to the Lord, the Rock of our salvation.

Let me ask you a few simple questions. Do you recognize God's hand in your life? Are you a five-talent person? a two-talent person? Do you wonder if you've been given even one talent? What are you doing with the talents that God has blessed you with?

Think about it. Your answers may reach into eternity. Your honesty with yourself will be a part of the stories that fill "your life books of glory to God."

BEGINNING TO UNDERSTAND

Let's randomly start with time. Your day has the same 24 hours that's been given to every other man, woman, and child. As an adult, you most likely decide how you will use these hours. If you are a young person, others may make a lot of such decisions for you. God understands this. Are your hours being used for your enjoyment—eating, sleeping, working, playing? Are you scheduling time for service in your church, your community, even in your neighborhood? Are you using some of these hours to bless those who are old and alone, little children, or perhaps someone who doesn't know God?

If you were to place your 24-hour schedule before God each day, would He stamp His seal of approval on it? Or might He suggest small changes that would enable you to make a meaningful difference in another life? What about time for Bible study and prayer? Are they a part of your successful Christian life?

Look at the funds God has blessed you with. Is it money that the Bible says is the root of all evil, or the love of money? Again, hold up your budgets, your purchases, and your projects to God. Can you look at His nail-scarred hands and say, "I can't afford to share my funds with the down-and-out people of this world"? Are you eager to help sponsor a Vacation Bible School or an evangelistic series? Unless the people around you have the opportunity to hear about Jesus, nothing else really matters. Are you generous in passing out literature or sharing magazines and books with people you come in contact with?

With both time and money, the possibilities seem almost limitless. But those are only two ways that we are blessed.

My favorite is the voice. Imagine singing (to shut-ins, babies, and children; in a choir or musical group); speaking (one-on-one, to a small group or class, at work, in the store, on a plane or in a car, preaching, teaching). You could be reading stories, sharing miracles, giving instructions, or praying, writing, laughing, or crying with others. You see, our voice makes all the difference between "Well done" and "I don't know you."

What about strength? I believe our cooking could be included in this group. Do you look for ways to bless others with the bounty from your kitchen? Does your diet, the food you share, or what others see you eat tell a story of good health and how to treat your body for a long and healthy life? Using your strength could mean running errands for God by supplying some of the needs of His earthly children. Volunteering. Building. The possibilities stretch into eternity.

Talk about health. Many have the gift of healing: doctors, nurses, therapists, and dentists use this gift to glorify God. This year our neighbors (doctor, nurse, and two college-age children) made yet another mission trip—blessing others with the gifts that God has given them.

I must not forget the gifts of prayer and listening. What a blessing to be able to recognize signs of sickness, pain, anger, or distress in another person and be filled with the desire to reach out to that person.

THE TRAP

In the story of the talents the saddest line went like

this: "And I was afraid, and went and hid your talent in the ground" (Matthew 25:25).

Fear plays havoc with our lives. How often have you been kept from joining something you might have enjoyed, or been good at, because of that one four-letter word? Could it be a fear of being ignored, laughed at, replaced, or unappreciated that has kept you or me from serving? Perhaps a fear of not being the best, of making a mistake, or of not being chosen sounds worse to you? Fear has as many sides as the people who possess it. Fear takes away our ability to respond to God's invitation to bless others.

What can we do to conquer such fear? Are we destined to stand helplessly by while another is given our talent?

That's the teeth in the trap of fear. When we bury a talent—put it away for any reason—our ability to use it is diminished. In such areas as singing, playing a musical instrument, teaching, preaching, even telling stories and praying, we become less and less gifted and more and more hesitant about getting involved. Just as muscles not used begin to atrophy, so our talents not used begin to lessen and disappear.

"Talents used are talents multiplied. Success is not the result of chance or of destiny; it is the outworking of God's own providence, the reward of faith and discretion, of virtue and persevering effort. The Lord desires us to use every gift we have; and if we do this, we shall have greater gifts to use" (*Christ's Object Lessons,* p. 353). No words can be plainer. The requirements for gaining talents are so simple yet so true. Still, we sit lifeless, watching and listening to others, afraid to take a step toward an adventure of faith and abundant blessings.

"Many who excuse themselves from Christian effort plead their inability for the work. But did God make them so incapable? No, never. This inability has been produced by their own inactivity and perpetuated by their deliberate choice. Already, in their own characters, they are realizing the result of the sentence, 'Take the talent from him'" (*Christ's Object Lessons,* p. 365).

How can God do it? How can He take me, once so sad and afraid, and send me to speak in churches and at retreats, to people I don't know but for whom I've already prayed?

~· **Chapter 6** ·~

THE ANSWER IS
SO SIMPLE—TO GOD

*"There is no fear in love; but perfect love
casts out fear, because fear involves torment. But he
who fears has not been made perfect in love" (1 John 4:18).*

Did you catch the antidote for fear? Four times in one verse the ugly word "fear" pokes up its terrifying head. Yet three times the same verse tells us where to turn. Again, we find a four-letter word capable of overpowering the tormentor "fear."

One word: love. "For God so loved the world . . ." (John 3:16). "Perfect love" can conquer fear every time. The Bible says, "By this we know love, because He laid down His life for us. And we also ought to lay down our lives for the brethren" (1 John 3:16).

It sounds simple. Yet it's the work of a lifetime. Study the Bible. Make "love" the theme of your study. Love's price? His life—your life. Give your life to Him. No matter if you are mocked and beaten. Remain calm if you are scorned and rejected. "Beloved, let us love one another, for love is of God; and everyone who loves is born of God and knows God. He who does not love does not know God, for God is love" (1 John 4:7, 8).

First God loved us. Now we must love God. We must love Him so much that we're willing to become one with Him. When we find that we long to make His wishes become our wishes, we know we're in love.

Yet, love is multifaceted; once we've fallen hopelessly in love with God, we begin to love others. Not because they deserve our love. In fact, we may not even know them. We love them because they are brothers and sisters for whom Christ died.

Suddenly, we do what we do, not out of guilt, but because a burning desire to serve others lives within us. We long to walk where Jesus walked. Our earthly mission is to be a blessing.

Gone are the jitters we often experience when we envision that we will fail. They are replaced with the promise that if we work for God, we cannot fail. You see, with God it is impossible to fail. We've just read that "God is love." First Corinthians 13:8 goes further: *"Love never fails. But whether there are prophecies, they will fail; whether there are tongues, they will cease; whether there is knowledge, it will vanish away."*

"And now abide faith, hope, love, these three; but the greatest of these is love" (verse 13).

ASKING GOD FOR A MIRACLE

One Sabbath afternoon I realized that God had given me everything He needed me to have to use me for His glory. That became a turning point in my life.

I humbly knelt by my favorite chair and gave my heart and life fully to Him. I wanted to hold nothing back. I threw my fear down at His feet and asked for a spirit of love and boldness.

The mustard seed of faith began to grow. How could I know that I could trust God? I'd read about how He said, "I say to you, ask, and it will be given to you; seek, and you will find; knock, and it will be opened to you. For everyone who asks receives, and he who seeks finds, and to him who knocks it will be opened" (Luke 11:9, 10).

I NEEDED A SMILE

A great desire burned in my heart. I needed a smile. That smile would come from the trust that God had our good (the good of our family) in the palm of His hand. He'd be there for us. That smile would come from a joy in service in whatever area He directed me to. That smile would come from a peace that passed all understanding. "Be anxious for nothing, but in everything by prayer and supplication, with thanksgiving, let your requests be made known to God; and the peace of God, which surpasses all understanding, will guard your hearts and minds through Christ Jesus" (Philippians 4:6, 7).

MAKE MY TALENT A SMILE

"Please, God, You know I'm having a problem with worry, and putting life on hold. You are stronger than these things. If You are the big God I read about, You can do anything. This one thing I ask. Please make me known as 'the smiling person.' Wherever I go, make people remember me as the woman who 'smiles all the time.' By this I will know that there is no one stronger than You. I will remember that nothing is stronger than You. Today I give my face to You. Make it over. Help me frown only if I take my face back from You."

I didn't stop with asking. When an extra moment developed, I studied everything I could find about a smile. Although Jesus was a man of sorrow, I read that children were drawn to Him. I found that His face "shone" because He spent so much time with His Father. How I longed to have a shining face. Perhaps that could come later.

What a challenge to read that even when I am worried or feel sad, I shouldn't let it show on my face (*The Adventist Home,* p. 432). The more I read, the more I fell in love with Jesus. How could one be altogether lovely without a smile or a peaceful face?

WHAT TO DO NEXT?

How would I handle my new smile? Could it be used to glorify God?

Again I knelt by my favorite chair and poured out my heart to God. "I'm a baby, a growing Christian, God, with a whole new talent. Today I'm going to make this vow to You. If anyone asks me to do something, something I can do with Your help, I will do it. You know, God, that I cannot play the piano. You gave that talent to my sisters. But quietly, only to You, I promise to being willing."

It seemed a safe prayer to pray. More than a year had passed since I had been asked to do anything at church.

As a safeguard, I refrained from telling Dennis. I could see no reason to take chances.

Less than a week later my first request came. "Ginger," said a dear sister in the church, "we never see you up front. Would you please give the mission story next week?"

I said "Yes!" What else could I say?

After lunch that day I told Dennis, my more experienced husband, the whole story. "What am I going to do?" I pleaded.

"There's a podium up there, so no one can see your knees knock. Just hold on to it, smile a lot, talk slowly, and you'll do fine."

It worked. The story seemed to go well, and I soon found myself beyond that challenge. Except that very next week, I was approached by someone else to tell the children's story for church.

What could I say? I said, "Yes!" and again sought my husband's advice on how to make it through this new assignment.

"Sit down on the steps with the children," he suggested. "That way, no one can see your knees knock. Take something up front in a paper bag. Kids love surprises. Use a funny voice, and they'll love your story."

It worked, and again I rejoiced in how good it was to work with God and Dennis.

A few uneventful weeks passed, and again I found myself faced with a challenge. This time it turned out to be the most active woman in the church.

"Ginger, I want to ask you something, but don't

answer now. I know you're quite shy, so just go home and pray about it."

"OK, Evelyna, go ahead and ask me."

"I don't want you to answer yet. I'll get your answer next week. I need you to have five minutes of the sermon in three weeks."

You got it. I said, "Yes!" They wanted me to talk about Christian education, and I believed in sacrificing for Christian education.

"YOU'VE STRETCHED ME A LOT, LORD"

Growth brings change and often makes one uncomfortable. Yet where would God's children be without growth? You and I would feel sad if our baby were never to develop the challenging skills of crawling, walking, talking, even crying.

Yet ever on my mind was "Slow down, God. Don't get too far ahead of me!"

I can hear God's chuckle: "Don't worry, My daughter; I've got some great surprises planned for you."

Chapter 7

THE UNWELCOME STRANGER

*"For He shall give His angels charge over you,
to keep you in all your ways" (Psalm 91:11).*

A ngel stories have always fascinated me. What would it take for God to send an angel in human form to you? Would an ordinary person recognize their angel? What if your angel came with a request that you felt was surely not from God?

Enough said about angels and their visits. My days were filled with children. Take children to school. Pick up children. My own two, plus six others at times—and all under age 8. The sewing and other tasks I'd once felt necessary were placed on the back burner. My days were filled with the nitty-gritty tasks of life. We got into a routine, and life rocked along.

You probably wouldn't call me unfriendly—just preoccupied. So that day, when the doorbell rang, I answered it with a bit of impatience. "May I help you?" I asked the tall stranger who stood there, smiling at me.

"Yes!" she replied. "I've got something I want you to do."

She had to be kidding. Couldn't she see? Didn't she know? I already had no extra time. I stood there, staring at her.

"I represent Avon. You've been chosen to sell it in your neighborhood."

I was incredulous. I told her that there was no Avon representative in the neighborhood, and that I certainly didn't want to be one.

"I know," she patiently replied. "That's why we've chosen you."

"Who's chosen me?" I asked impatiently. I really didn't know many women in the neighborhood, and I couldn't imagine any of them choosing me.

She skirted the issue and kept on talking. "We'll want you to start right away. I'll be back in a week with your case. Just have a check for $25 made out to Avon when I return."

"Wait!" I couldn't believe her nerve. "I don't want to sell Avon. I'm not a salesperson, and I already have my hands full with babysitting."

"Just ask your husband. I'll be back in a week. I know you'll do a good job."

She turned around and walked away. I closed the door, still wondering about the whole thing. I doubted she'd even return.

WE'LL SEE WHAT HE SAYS . . .

What was she thinking? Dennis wanted me to stay at home with the boys. I wanted to be at home. I cooked a special meal and stewed. *I don't know how they get any-*

one to do that job! Who would want to go to the homes of perfect strangers and try to sell them who-knows-what?

I knew what he would say . . .

Dinner over, I decided the time was right to tell Dennis about my strange visitor. A bit taken aback, I described how she just wouldn't take no for an answer. I almost laughed when I told him she had told me to ask my husband. "Can you believe her? She really made a mistake saying that."

"No! I think it's a great idea! You need to get out. You can sell in the evening while I'm home to stay with the boys."

You could have knocked me over with a feather. What had he said?

God and I talked that night. I trusted Dennis, and always appreciated his advice in regard to my life. But sell Avon? A few days later the check I felt we could little afford lay by the door.

Exactly a week later the doorbell rang; I opened the front door to the tall stranger, who smiled at me once again. She stood there holding the scary flower-covered bag I would be using to sell Avon.

Being in a state of shock and hoping the whole thing would just go away, I stood there quietly as she took my check, quickly described my territory, and left me standing in a daze. As she turned to leave, she turned back and said, "By the way, if you want more houses, the apartments to your northeast are available. Feel free to go there anytime."

One thing I knew for sure—I would not need more homes!

A NEW CHALLENGE

Never underestimate the power of prayers. Whose prayers—my mother's, my family's, Dennis's family's?—I cannot say. Someone had chosen me to do something I did not want to do. The best way seemed to get on with it and spend no more time fretting.

THE WAY OF PRAYERS

Each day I prayed for God's blessing on our family. I gave Him my family and "my face." Then I asked God to return us to California. We had been told "three years." Now five had passed, and we were still in faraway Nebraska. Try as I might, I could not make sense of why my prayers were not being answered. So I prayed harder and more often. "God, You know the desires of my heart. You can make them happen. I believe You want what is best for us. Thank You in advance for what You are going to do."

And I began to make the rounds of the neighborhood with my new Avon bag. The first thing to strike me was the friendliness of the neighbors. Most greeted me with "Well, come on in. We haven't had an Avon person in a long time. Let's see what you have."

My biggest surprise and joy came when I attended the first biweekly meeting for the Avon representatives of our district. More than 100 of us attended, and I enjoyed their lively spirit, the laughter, and the new friend I had made—Mary, who was the representative in the next territory. Soon we were enjoying a fast friendship. Her love for God seemed to be something she really enjoyed sharing, and it didn't embarrass her in the least.

I, on the other hand, being young and less active in my church, seldom mentioned God and my religion during our times together.

So it caught me by surprise the day that Bob, Mary's husband, called to tell me that she was seriously sick and in the hospital. "I think she'd like a visit," he said as he ended the call.

NOW WHAT DO I DO?

My pastor father had felt right at home in a hospital visiting a patient. I did not. With a little persuasion Dennis and the boys drove along with me—they'd wait in the car, and we'd go to the park afterward. My purse felt a bit heavy with those three small paperback sharing books that Dennis had suggested I leave with Mary.

I hadn't thought about all the people who would also be visiting at that time. How awkward I felt among those strangers. A couple minutes of chitchat, and I was on my way out, walking down the hall at a good clip, when a voice in my head startled me.

"You forgot to leave the books," it reminded me.

That's OK. I'll leave them next time—if she's here that long.

"Go back and leave the books!" The voice came again, stronger this time.

How could I go back? This couldn't be the right thing to do! I'd be so embarrassed breaking into all those friends and family members again. I turned, and this time slowly retraced my steps to her room.

"I'm sorry, Mary. I forgot to leave these three little books. I know you're not feeling well, and it looks like you don't have too much time to read, but I'll leave them anyway." With that said, I fled.

A few days later she smiled as I entered her now-quiet room. It seemed as though Mary had been waiting for me. She beckoned me to have a seat in the chair closest to her bed. "You know," she began, "I almost died three times Saturday night. Things got so bad that they just decided to keep the lights on. Nurses were in and out at all hours poking and prodding me. Then, when all had grown quiet, yet another nurse slipped in.

" 'Excuse me,' she said. 'Could I borrow those little books?'

"I nodded my head yes and slipped quietly back into my world of pain. They finally got me stabilized, and I slept fitfully. About sunrise the same nurse, the one who had taken the books, slipped into my room again.

" 'Thank you for sharing,' she whispered. 'I don't know why I was in your room. I work in another building. I guess I saw your light on. You see, I had planned to commit suicide last night. Instead, I read your books and found hope. They saved my life.' "

I reached to take Mary's hand, and she continued.

"Ginger, that nurse then turned and left. I have no idea who she was. I guess God knew that she would need your books."

A BIGGER VISION
Visiting more than 50 homes every two weeks kept

me busy; yet somewhere deep inside I felt a nudging toward those apartments northeast of us. Finally I could stand it no longer and made my decision to begin visiting each one to see if there were any interests there.

As weeks turned into months, I became an expected friend and visitor into many of the homes in the neighborhood. Instead of being a chore, I began to enjoy getting out and visiting these interesting women. But beginning another territory cold turkey wasn't easy. *What if these women aren't friendly?*

All went quite well for most of the apartments. I began on the second floor, made a couple of new friends, and kept on going. I'd almost finished. The last two apartments had outdoor entrances off the back side. I started to make my way to the first one, where I saw an older woman standing on her patio. Smiling, I headed toward it. Then it happened! I had taken only a couple of steps in that direction when suddenly a voice screeched at me, "Go away, miss. Just leave me alone! Don't ever come to my house!"

I fled. I wouldn't venture any closer that day or any other day. Each time I chanced to be near that apartment, I gave it a wide berth. That unfriendly woman would not have an opportunity to humiliate me again. I never wanted to talk to her, see her, or even set foot again onto her property. I felt sure of that. Had I only known . . .

A NEW FOCUS AND A NEW PRAYER

A spirit of discontent does not come from God, of

that I am sure. He bids us, "Trust in the Lord with all your heart, and lean not on your own understanding" (Proverbs 3:5).

We often reply, "Sure, God, I will; and I do trust You. But let me tell You the best way to handle a situation like this."

Suddenly I found myself focusing less and less on "being" in Omaha and more and more in "making a difference in the lives of others." I took my meager Avon profits and invested in sending a Christian sharing magazine subscription to every woman in my neighborhood that I had a relationship with. They had so many questions to ask me. Our relationships developed and grew. For the first time, I couldn't imagine leaving these neighbors I'd grown to cherish.

Where once my prayers were "Please give me the desires of my heart," they grew little by little to focus on "Give them (my neighbors who don't even know about You) a clearer understanding of You. Let my life be a picture of Your love. Amen."

Lest my prayers settle into sameness, at times I'd humbly say something like this: "I've got it, Lord. You know I'm a fast learner. You don't need to worry about me. This new life of mine should last for a lifetime. You can focus on others now. I'm perfectly fine. Let's not change anything else. Thank You, Lord. Amen."

"Do you love Me? . . . Feed My sheep"

"Lady! Oh, lady! I've been watching you." The voice caught me by surprise. "You always go around my apartment and never stop by. Come here, please. I want to talk to you."

Could it have been a momentary lapse? Perhaps my need to hurry had caused me to forget my exact location at that moment. In a heartbeat I recognized that voice—I'd wandered into the forbidden territory of that first-floor outside apartment on the left.

My hair stood on end. Fear gripped me. Had I stepped on her precious lawn? Did my smile offend her? I felt trapped. What could I do but murmur a prayer and walk forward toward my doom?

This time she smiled. A look of regret with a hint of sadness added to my discomfort.

"Please sit," she instructed me. "You don't know how many times I've wished you'd be my friend since that terrible day I spoke so harshly to you. I'm sorry. You just don't understand."

I did not. I just wanted to be out of there.

"That terrible afternoon was the worst day of my life. You see, I'd just returned home after having both of my breasts removed. I was without family and friends and wanted to die. The pain seemed more than I could bear. So I lashed out at you, a perfect stranger."

If only I had known the reason for her anger that fateful afternoon. How much this precious woman had needed someone to hold her in her darkest hour! My prayers could have given her comfort and hope. I had not walked in her shoes and yet I had judged her. Lord, I'm the one who needs forgiveness. "Forgive us our debts, as we forgive our debtors."

More likely God wanted to get my attention and

open my eyes to the wonders of friendship and grace that afternoon. *You cannot know everything, Ginger. If you err, err on the side of love and forgiveness. Do not despair. Love her now. Feed My sheep.*

And love her I did. My prayers for her ascended often from that day forward. My eyes were opened to possibilities I'd never imagined possible.

Change was on the way. Life cannot remain stagnant. But that day I learned a lesson that would forever influence the way I would view arrogant and unfriendly strangers.

~· Chapter 8 ·~

"YOUR WILL—NOT MINE"

"Then you will call upon Me and go and pray to Me, and I will listen to you. And you will seek Me and find Me, when you search for Me with all your heart" (Jeremiah 29:12, 13).

Five years had passed, and still we occupied that little house on the side of a hill in Omaha, Nebraska. Many had been the time I'd pleaded with God to "take me home to California." Now busy with a husband, the boys, and Avon, not to mention doing more at church, I'd almost put aside that burning desire to move on. Almost . . .

Life looked good. Dennis and I had put our heads together. No more "sadness" when he traveled. Instead, the boys and I would make a plan. We'd do fun things, cook great food, and live life just as it came, with gusto. I thanked God often for His patience and the love of a wonderful husband. Who could ask for anything more?

WHEN YOU LEAST EXPECT IT

Dennis worked hard and, as a result, received a promotion to be the manager of the Omaha branch. How proud I felt. Yes, he'd still be traveling; but, as we had over the years, the boys and I would sometimes go along, and together we'd make a difference.

Neither of us had expected the phone call that came, once again, out of the blue. This time it had to do with me. The home office wanted me to work as Dennis's secretary. We had already decided that I would be a stay-at-home mother. It wasn't a hard decision—we said, "No!"

They asked again—and again.

We prayed about it. Why wouldn't they just take no for an answer? We *could* use the money. Finally we came up with a plan. Our younger son, Dony, was now in school. If they would let me work part-time—mother's hours—this job could give us the best of both worlds.

We expected an immediate answer.

One week passed. Two weeks. They say ignorance is bliss. But I had been given this seed of hope—the two of us working together. Was it now to be dashed? *God, I had been so happy, so content. Why did they hold out this carrot of hope, just to dash it as soon as we got interested?*

Into the third week my mind knew the answer would not be what we had hoped. Yet how could I give up hope? Why would I hold on to the impossible?

Again I knelt by my favorite rocker. "God, I know You give and You take away. I praise Your name. Nothing can take away my happiness. I trust You to do what is for our best. I accept Your will, not mine."

The ringing phone pulled me back into the present. Who could be calling?

Rising, I got to the phone just in time.

"You got the job!" Dennis beamed into the phone.

I could almost see the joy in the face of my wonderful husband. "They say you can start immediately. We can still travel together as a family—as long as your work gets done. You can set your own hours."

What a celebration we had that night. "And Lord, to think that I didn't want any changes made to my life . . . You really are something else! Let me do this to Your glory."

ACCEPTING GOD'S PROMISES

What does God mean by "asking"? How shall I "seek"? When will I "find"? And how will it be "opened to me"? I have come to believe that for each of us this process is as individual as we ourselves are. God "knows our frame" and works with each of us individually.

My asking for "a move" had ceased. I reveled in this new path that God had us walking. Finally, instead of steep hills or dark valleys, we walked in the sun. During those first years in Omaha I only endured. Slowly, acceptance came. Finally, for the past two years I had come to embrace each day as a gift from God. God's gifts were wonderful. What more could we want? Then the phone rang again.

WE NEED YOU BACK IN MOUNTAIN VIEW

By now prices had skyrocketed in California. What were we to do? How could we ever afford for me to work only part-time? What would we do with Buffy, our cocker spaniel? Most apartments that we and our two boys would want to live in would not allow pets. *God, Your timing seems all wrong. We sooo can't afford to move. What are You thinking? We're willing, but how will You ever pull this off?*

Our tickets were bought. Only a couple more days, and we'd be on the plane to California with a mission to find a place to live. (How would one find the right place in only three days?) Just this week we'd placed our house on the market. *(Sorry, God, we remember how You placed us in this house more than seven years ago—only then I had been kicking and screaming. You even made it possible for us to buy it. Now look at it—it's beautiful, thanks to a talented, hard-working husband who came equipped with the skills of building and remodeling. The boys will surely miss their forts—one built in the basement for winter and spring; the other outside for summer and fall.)* How would it all work out?

We need you more in Nashville, Tennessee

We were willing. God is able. Did we return to California? No. The tickets to California were never used. Instead, they were cashed in. God led us to Southern Publishing Association in Nashville, Tennessee. And the road we traveled continued to bend and turn.

A rental house awaited us there. A place used for just such purposes. Each day, after Dennis went to work and the boys went to school, I went house hunting. Weeks passed, and nothing that met our specifications—country setting, nice-size yard, some trees, a prayer rock for me (and Lord, please make it two-story, and affordable on one income [or one and a half incomes])—materialized. Then, when all seemed hopeless, I found it! The house—a new house (OK, perhaps a bit small), in a quiet neighborhood (it wasn't on a main thoroughfare), that we could (almost) afford.

Dennis had lots of misgivings about purchasing this place. His biggest objection was that it seemed too far away from his job and the boys' school. But I knew the house must be the right one. Surely God wouldn't have led me to this special little house if it weren't meant for us!

I begged, I pleaded, and I won. Dennis gave in. We wrote out a deposit check. That left only one more hurdle. We needed to sell our house in Omaha. Our real estate agent added a clause to the purchase agreement, saying that the house would remain on the market and that if the sellers found another buyer, we would have three days to get the money and purchase it.

The 20-minute drive to our temporary home seemed longer than it should have been. I wanted to expound on the joy of "almost" owning a new house. Dennis seemed lost in deep thought. Finally he spoke: "I really hope we haven't made a bad decision. This place is so far away . . ." What if my "want" to buy this house had overtaken our real "need" to purchase the right house?

Arriving home, we walked into the kitchen to a ringing phone. Dennis's one-sided phone conversation went something like this: "They didn't? You're going to tear up our deposit check? You've never had this happen before?" What were they talking about?

That day the seller rejected our offer. He did not want to wait for his money. We, on the other hand, got our deposit money back and didn't make a terrible mistake. A few weeks later God led us to another place, one that more than met our list of "wants" and "needs."

"I'M READY TO FOLLOW—NOT LEAD"

Two years later Southern Publishing Association merged with the Review and Herald. Two more moves came in quick succession—to Silver Spring, Maryland, and then on to Hagerstown, Maryland. Despite the trials and hardships we faced during those busy years, our faith grew. There were more miracles mingled with challenges. Some days we would feel alone; others brought profound blessings. One day a phone call came inviting me to apply for a mother's-hours job at the General Conference, which I didn't even know I wanted.

God remained faithful. I kept my vow to speak for Him, to use any talent I could recognize. If I were asked to play the piano, I could not do that. When someone asked me to write my worship material into a story, I knew I "could not" do that. So, of course, I said, "No, I'm not interested."

God does not seem to understand the language of "No!" During the following weeks Penny Wheeler asked me to write. Marie Spangler asked and asked again. Jocey Fay and Aileen Sox just wouldn't drop their challenge to "write something."

Finally, again, I said "Yes" to God. I slowly began to write; small at first, doing my best to follow God's leading. There were so many "encouragers" along the way. During those first trying times I couldn't imagine this was what God wanted me to do. Today I find no greater joy than inviting others to use their God-given talent of writing to bless others. What a pleasure to be an "encourager" for the Lord!

THE CHALLENGE

I never wanted to be a speaker. Being part of the audience seemed safe. All those people had to make one nervous. Yet invitations and opportunity came just often enough to keep me unsettled.

So that day, after speaking to my fellow workers at the Review and Herald, my heart sang when our son Doug came to me with a hug and the much-appreciated words "You did good, Mom." I gathered the compliment like a bouquet that belonged to God and felt a warm glow.

Instead of walking away, he continued: "Someday, Mom, you will get up and speak without reading. You will just talk to the people. It will be a lot better."

I was floored. What could he be thinking? Didn't he know I had already been stretched to the limit? Didn't he know?

Never underestimate the power of God. Often, as I stand to teach what I've learned about speaking in public, I wonder at the way God uses the weak and fearful to teach others. To any who are willing, He grants the privilege of spreading His message of service.

Encouraging others—what a talent. To those who have been there for me, and there are always those in any audience who are encouragers, I say, "Thank you. God will reward you for a job well done. Continue to sit near the front. Smile and nod your head in agreement. Pray for those who are before you. The sphere of your service will spread far. You are a friend to many and a servant of God."

Chapter 9

When God Says "Go" and "Do"—
What Will You Do?

*A friend once told me, "When God asks me
to do something for Him, I remember Jonah and
I quickly say 'Yes!' You know, I just can't swim that well."*

For more than 15 years I have traveled, spoken, written, and shared God's love in more ways than I ever could have imagined. Growth doesn't happen overnight. Growth comes slowly, moment by moment, year by year: a lifetime of experiences built on faith, trust, love, and hope.

Growth comes through praying, pleading, and listening to the still small voice. It includes times of sorrow, misunderstanding, and life-changing setbacks that shake you through and through.

Growth comes during high times, bringing memories of exceptional love and unmerited acceptance. These experiences lie ingrained in the deepest valleys of your innermost being. Unexpected friendships and unselfish acts of love add warmth and encouragement to sustain you through the darkest nights and the most difficult days.

Serving God wholeheartedly may take you to places

you never wanted to go. It can cause you to meet new people you can't imagine you ever wanted to meet. Loneliness may hound you. You may face criticism, receive praise, or experience the disturbing fate of being totally ignored. Jesus experienced all these and more. He asks us to follow in His footsteps. Can we do less?

THE JOURNEY IS UP TO YOU

Place your name in each of these verses, along with their instruction and promises. These promises, made to others long ago, still stand for us today. Commenting on 1 Kings 11:38, my Bible commentary says, "Jeroboam was a young man of promise. He had outstanding abilities that would make him a powerful leader and a strong influence for good, if he would walk in the ways of the Lord. God is not partial, but grants His blessings to all who are faithful to Him" (*The Seventh-day Adventist Bible Commentary,* vol. 2, p. 787).

These blessings are every bit as available to you and me as they were to men and women of Bible times. How, then, do we make God's blessings part of our daily lives? *"Then it shall be, if you heed all that I command you, walk in My ways, and do what is right in My sight, to keep My statutes and My commandments" (1 Kings 11:38).*

How often has God blessed you? How many times have you recognized God's blessings—His watch care to you and your family—and taken them for granted? What an awesome tool of awareness, if each of us would keep a "book of blessings"! How much we forget, unable to share with others, because the stories grow dim!

During a recent women's retreat I encouraged those attending to begin their own special blessings book. That evening one of the women attending felt ill and returned home. During their family worship the family of three sat discussing the blessings book idea. Their teenage daughter laughed at the idea of her parents really keeping such a journal. The father suddenly reached out and drew the daughter to himself in a bear hug. "We will do it!" he responded. "And you, my daughter, will be the first blessing we place in it."

The question is not "Have we been blessed?" The questions are: "What are we doing about these blessings? Will they build our faith? Will they burn like a light in our lives, showing others the glorious character of God?"

Within the following pages you will find stories of praise and honor to a God who can and will do above what we can ever think or imagine. He can make the wounded whole again, make the sick able to stand and walk. Cause the blind to see. He can take you and me—weary, alone, afraid, unworthy, and unable—and make of us a bright light in a dark night. Through Him we can be a blessing where only curses and discontent seem to dwell. Only God can find what is hopelessly lost and bring rejoicing and celebration.

Journey with me a little while, before our roads fork and separate. We'll walk with God toward complete surrender. In each of the following stories you will see the tenderness of God, our Creator and Abba God, who weeps with us and shares our burdens—often by bringing us love in human form. The One who listens when we cannot be still, who handles us with patience when we ourselves would take over and "get something done."

These stories are shared for two reasons: (1) to give glory to God; (2) to increase our faith.

Today I understand, as never before, why John wrote, *"And there are also many other things that Jesus did, which if they were written one by one, I suppose that even the world itself could not contain the books that would be written"* (John 21:25). Each moment that you and I live can be written as a testimony to God's incredible love, grace, and response to each of His children. The stories that follow are all true. Many of them happened to me in this incredible journey we call life. Others have been shared by family, friends, or strangers who realized and wanted to share the awesomeness of God.

~· Chapter 10 ~·

"I CAN'T DO THIS, GOD"

*"I commend to you Phoebe our sister, who is a servant
of the church in Cenchrea, that you may receive her in the Lord
in a manner worthy of the saints, and assist her in whatever
business she has need of you; for indeed she has
been a helper of many and of myself also" (Romans 16:1, 2).*

Many months went by before I really understood the nature of traveling, promoting, and speaking. Wasn't it just part of life? So many people would suggest to me, "Going to new places and meeting new people must be so very exciting." Others would remind me, "You are so blessed."

Yet each time I returned from a weekend, sometimes a week on the road, I would find myself tired and feeling "used up." I'd wonder, *Why is this happening to me?* Then I'd go to work, sit down at my desk, and again face the task of editing *Celebration* magazine. What a struggle!

"I've lost my creativity, Lord. Am I weak? I think I'm following Your will."

Monthly, as the issues came and went, I'd wonder how to handle these "day after" times, when I felt drained and overwhelmed.

On a Monday morning, tired from traveling into the night, I once again faced my computer. Nothing came.

How would I put this issue together? All seemed hopeless. Feelings of doubt and discouragement overwhelmed me.

Unable to hold back my tears any longer, I dropped to my knees facing my chair and buried my face in my arms. "It's too hard, Lord." I cried. "Today this magazine is a mountain I just can't get over. I'm alone and overwhelmed. Show me that You care. Please replace these feelings of tiredness and despair with Your Spirit of peace and joy."

Moments passed. Slowly peace filled the places where only pain had been. Tears spent, I again sat before my computer intent on focusing on the tasks at hand.

The shrill ring of the telephone brought me into full reality. *Who would be calling me this early in the morning? Would they be able to tell I had been crying?*

"Ginger, you don't know me. I'm from [she named a faraway city]. I've got a text for you today. It's found in Romans 16. It says, *'I commend to you Phoebe our sister, who is a servant of the church in Cenchrea, that you may receive her in the Lord in a manner worthy of the saints, and assist her in whatever business she has need of you; for indeed she has been a helper of many and of myself also.'*

"Ginger, you are Phoebe. I am praying for you today. I'm holding up your hands. I am your encourager!"

She prayed with me then. She prayed a beautiful prayer of hope and thanksgiving. Then she was gone. God had been right there with me. He understood. He knew I needed "an angel" to strengthen me. The faithful ministrations of my wonderful friend replaced my low supply of faith and gave me renewed courage. That long-ago day God sent a wonderful sister to bless me with a vision of His ever-present care over His earthly children.

A few weeks later I found myself listening to Bill Pierce on *Night Sounds*. He spoke of "winging my way through the late-night sky."

He had my attention. Wasn't that what I found myself doing so often lately?

"This weekend," he began, "I found myself wide awake, thinking of people I had just ministered to. There, sitting in a darkened plane, flying across the night sky, for the first time I realized that when we give ourselves to others, we give all we have—we empty ourselves."

As he spoke in his deep and soothing voice, I knew his words must be for me.

"Remember this whenever you spend time doing what you love—talking to others, preaching, sharing, and caring. When you empty yourself, you must be filled again before you have anything else to give away. Take time for yourself—to reconnect with God. Take time to refill your soul with His wonderful love."

Remember. Refill. Rejoice. Reconnect. Don't return home without doing them.

WHEN GOD CHANGED THE PLAN

The trip to the northeastern part of the United States as a speaker for a leadership training event had been wonderful. The woman who met me at the airport had been a real friend and help to me during the whole weekend.

The only downside had been that a cold, which I

had felt coming on when I left home, had suddenly hit me hard. Sunday noon I shared last hugs with those I'd grown to care about, and we gathered together in a circle one last time to ask for traveling mercies for me and for all the others who were now ready to leave. My eagerness to return home had to be curbed since my flight to Baltimore wouldn't be leaving until evening.

I assured Alice and her husband, my gracious hosts, that they could just drop me off at the airport—that I didn't mind being early. They declined, assuring me that they had plenty of time and wanted to take me for an afternoon of sightseeing.

One of the places they were excited about showing me was Alice's oldest brother's home—the ancestral home where she and all her siblings had been born. I've always enjoyed looking at houses—old and new. When it turned out that he was not home, we were all a bit disappointed. Then, just as we were leaving, her brother drove up. Instead of going in, she hesitated. "It would be fun to show you around now that he's home, but I feel as though we need to keep going."

Early in the afternoon Alice made a surprising announcement: "We're near the airport, Ginger; let's see if we can get you on an early flight."

"That would be good." The idea was exciting. "But I probably wouldn't be allowed to get on, even if a flight were going."

We walked into the small terminal just as they were announcing over the loudspeaker that the 2:30 flight to Baltimore was "now loading."

"Go, get on it," she encouraged me.

"I couldn't possibly make it," I countered. "I haven't even checked in. Even if I made it, my suitcase couldn't possibly get on. And besides, Dennis won't be in Baltimore until an hour and a half later."

"Go, Ginger. What's Dennis's phone number? I'll call him."

As I boarded the plane I glanced back at my new friend. Her back was to me as she stood at the pay phone. *What are the chances she can get to him early?* I wondered as I boarded the plane. I had no trouble answering my own question. *There was little to no chance he would be there early to meet me!*

What a joy to be back on the ground. Flying with a stopped-up head was the pits. I'd people-watch after I checked for my "missing" suitcase.

How my suitcase also managed to get onto that plane in the five-minute window I gave them, I can only surmise. Just for kicks, I walked out to see if Dennis had received the call. Nothing . . . or were those his tail-lights leaving the waiting area? Yes, it was. A few minutes later he came around again.

As we drove away from the terminal, I looked at my watch in amazement and announced to Dennis, "Do you realize we are driving away at exactly the time I should have been boarding my original plane? What a blessing . . ."

ONE MORE THING TO DO

"Dennis, I'm feeling a bit peaked, but we need to take Shadow, our collie, for a walk as soon as we set the suitcase inside. You know how much he enjoys getting out and running."

Despite his misgivings about my state of health, we went.

Partway into the walk a car passed us, driving very slowly. Inside, an older man and woman looked lost and afraid. We watched in amazement as another car zipped by us and began to crowd the first one.

"What are those guys doing?" Dennis wanted to know.

"It looks like they are up to no good." I responded.

We both stopped to watch in horror as the event played out. At the next and last farm driveway the first car turned around. The second went on to the dead end, made a three-point turn, and also came back toward us.

As the first car pulled alongside us the woman pleaded, "Please help us. They are going to kill us."

By then the second car had come alongside the first one.

"You cut us off," one man shouted, as the three men raised their fists.

"Leave them alone," Dennis addressed the second car. "We're taking care of these folks."

To our surprise, the second car sped off.

"We were so afraid they would kill us. We didn't mean to get in their way. We were going to a funeral and got lost. If you had not been right here . . ." Both of them were clearly shaken. "We'll be fine now. You saved our lives."

God's impeccable timing. If we had arrived at the

terminal even five minutes later, the flight would have been gone already. Then I experienced another brief wait while Dennis made another loop around the airport, waiting for me to arrive. And now we understood my need to take a walk the minute we returned home.

Yes, that day we experienced a bit of heaven on earth. For in Isaiah we are told: "Before they call, I will answer" (Isaiah 65:24). God, Your plans are impeccable.

Chapter 11

"I'M AFRAID I WON'T BE SAVED"

"Those who sow in tears shall reap in joy,
He who continually goes forth weeping, bearing seed
for sowing, shall doubtless come again with
rejoicing, bringing his sheaves with him" (Psalm 126:5, 6).

So many things in life reveal our true feelings. The sadness or smile on our face and the tone of our voice are good indicators. Even our stance and our motions give large clues. The words she put on paper told me that this unknown stranger needed someone to talk to. Finding her phone number was easy, and I soon had her on the line.

"Is this Kathy?"★ I asked as a woman's voice came on the phone.

"Yes; who is this?"

"I'm Ginger Church with *Celebration* magazine. I got your letter today, and I wanted to talk to you. You sounded sad, and I wondered if I could help."

"It's just . . . I don't think that I'll be saved. You know, I've never seen anyone baptized because of me. I won't have any stars in my crown. I won't be able to go to heaven."

I understood her grief. I too had heard many people

say that only those who had "stars" in their crowns would be allowed to enter heaven. How often I had wondered about my own "stars."

Then suddenly I remembered my computer-savvy boys telling me that I would be awed and amazed at what an ordinary computer could do. "Mom, you just type in the name of a person, and lots of times you can find out all kinds of things about that individual." If an ordinary computer could do that, what could God's awesome system do?

"Have you ever been a mother?" I asked her.

"Yes."

"What about a Sabbath school leader or teacher? Have you worked with Community Services or served as a deaconess? What about working with Pathfinders or in a Vacation Bible School?"

"Yes, yes, and yes," she responded. But I've never stood at the baptismal tank and watched as someone I studied with was baptized."

I began to talk to her about computers here on earth and how we can look almost anyone up and find out so much about them. As I talked I heard a sound like crying. "Are you all right?" I asked my new friend. "Do you want to tell me a story?"

"I haven't thought of it in that way, but a few months ago I got a call from someone I hadn't seen for more than 40 years. You see, Charlotte and I were in college together, and our rooms shared a bathroom—we were bathmates.

"One day as I returned to my room after my last

class, I found Charlotte lying on her bed, crying as though her heart would break. I didn't know what to do. It hurt me to see her so sad. So I did the only thing I could think of to do—I sat down on the bed beside her, put my arms around her, and cried with her.

"After almost an hour had gone by, Charlotte had cried all her tears. She slowly dried her eyes, and told me she was pregnant and would have to leave school. I never saw her or heard from her again until just a short time ago. I must have sounded surprised to hear from her after all this time, although I did remember her well."

"What she said next will be forever etched into my mind. 'Kathy, you probably don't even remember me. I just wanted you to know that I have just received one of the highest awards our country can give for helping unwed mothers. You know, I always have done for them what you did for me. I sit down by them, put my arms around them, and cry with them.'"

"Blessed are you who hunger now, for you shall be filled. Blessed are you who weep now, for you shall laugh" (Luke 6:21).

LINDA'S STORY

The Review and Herald Publishing Association would soon be holding a stress seminar and had asked me to be a part of the team. I would serve as a team facilitator. The main speaker would present his material; then we would divide those attending into small groups.

At home my family and I began to kid about the "stressed-out seminars" I would be taking part in. We already worked nine and a half hours a day, so adding two more would make for some pretty long days.

The first evening there was a good attendance, and all went well, except for one thing—the man who wrote the seminar gave the seminar, which left no time that evening for small groups. What a disappointment. I wanted to do something.

The second night was like the first. The man who wrote the seminar gave the seminar, and he left no time for the small groups. Why had I wasted my time? Prospects for small-group participation didn't look very good for the rest of the two-week event.

The third evening I had already spent some time talking to the Lord beforehand. "What am I to do—just sit there and do nothing?"

A strong impression came to me to get to know the attendees. I felt that I should sit somewhere other than with my friends. And the third night went as before. I sat until I could sit no more; then I got up and went out into an adjoining larger room. From there I could see the lobby of the Review. Suddenly I noticed a lone woman sitting on the couch, face red, unable to stop her weeping.

"Who is that and why is she crying?" I asked another woman on the team.

"She's been here all three nights, and she can't stop crying. We are just leaving her alone."

We had just printed an entire issue of *Celebration* on the subject of grief. Surely this troubled woman needed a friend.

"Hi, my name is Ginger." *Now, where do I go from here?* I said the only thing that came to my mind. "You don't look very happy."

"I'm not! I'm going to die!" she wept.

Whoa . . . this isn't going very well!

Suddenly the thought came into my mind: *Talk to her about the eight laws of health.*

"What's your name?"

"Linda." More tears and wiping of eyes.

"Well, Linda, do you like to eat fruits and vegetables?"

"No! I hate those things." *Sniff, sniff.* "I just eat junk food."

"Do you like to walk?"

"I can't walk. I just lie in bed." A crying break. "I can hardly make it to the kitchen."

"Do you like to drink water?"

"No, I just drink pop and beer."

Things were looking hopeless. Did I dare go on?

"Do you know Jesus?"

With that the tears really began to flow. Finally Linda was able to reply. "I don't know Jesus. He doesn't even like me." Another pause for crying. "Well, maybe He does a little bit. When Jason—he's my common-law husband—drives us too fast on the motorcycle, Jesus has the police pull him over."

I asked her if she had any children. She answered that she had two. Her 9-year-old belonged to her and her first husband. That man had just died of cancer, and this was the reason for her sorrow. Somehow she felt that she too would have to die so that Jason, the man she currently lived with, could be saved. Her other daughter, a 2-year-old, was uncontrollable. She felt that she was a terrible mother and that neither girl liked her.

Having come up with total negatives in all areas, I searched my mind for what to do next. I told Linda that God did love her and that He had sent me to be her friend. Suddenly I got an idea.

"Linda," I said, "I am going to call you twice every day—at 10:00 a.m. and at 2:00 p.m. When you answer the phone, I'm going to say, 'Hi, Linda. This is Ginger. Are you drinking your water?' You can just answer 'Yes!' and then I will hang up."

I explained to her that we all need eight glasses a day to be really healthy. Then I added something that my mother had taught me as a child. "And you know, Linda, if you are drinking enough water, your urine will be clear."

I held Linda's hand just before the meeting closed, and asked God to bless her and her family and to take away her sorrow. The next morning I began my calling. Always she answered "Yes!" when I asked her about the water. I then said, "That's wonderful," and would hang up.

A FEW NIGHTS LATER

The next meeting I asked another team member to take notes for me, and I went out and sat with Linda. Still crying—still looking like she would die. We talked about how her older daughter had been molested and her baby "swore" all the time. (Later I would find out how true and complete that statement was.)

88

Just before the time for the breakout groups, I handed Linda some fun stickers. "Here's what I want you to do, Linda. In the morning, try to get out of bed and mix up a small batch of cookies. You can put the dough in the refrigerator while you go back and lie down. (Linda was extremely overweight, and I could imagine the vastness of her problems.) As soon as you get a small amount of energy, I want you to go back into the kitchen and bake just two cookies—one for each daughter. While they are baking, write each girl a note telling them how much you love them. Then put a few stickers on the notes and give each girl your gift of love."

We finally did have the small groups. As we sat down, one of the women in my group took my hand and asked, "Would you pray with me the way you did with the crying woman on the couch?" What a joy!

A REALLY HARD QUESTION

About halfway through the seminar Linda found me in a small room and asked a question that must have been burning in her mind. Linda had been brought to this event by Jason's Adventist sister.

"Melissa says that if I love God, I will leave Jason. What do you say?"

I knew Linda had lived with Jason as his common-law wife for more than eight years. He was the father of her younger daughter. How could I answer such a question? I silently sent a petition heavenward, "Lord, give me words to say. I do not want to wound Linda any more. You died for her. Give me wisdom."

ASK GOD FOR A MIRACLE

Suddenly the words of my friend Jeris Bragan came
to my mind. *Ginger, God asks us to be "fishers of men." He
does not ask us to clean the fish!*

I smiled at Linda and responded, "Linda, God has asked
me to be your friend. That is what I want to be. If God
wants you to leave Jason, He will tell you."

ARE YOU DRINKING YOUR WATER?

Day after day I made those calls. Linda always had a
positive answer. One day I was surprised to hear her respond, "I have told 20 other women what you told me
about water, and they are all drinking water too. And
Ginger, we all have clear urine!"

Linda came to the Review for every seminar. She
never stopped crying, and she never came in to hear one
of the seminars. Each night I would sit with her and hold
her hand. We talked of many things. I shared with her
how children become what we call them. Soon Linda re-
ported that she no longer called her younger daughter
"bad names."

As time went on, Linda started walking every day. She
organized a group of women who went swimming at the
Holiday Inn pool on a regular basis. "Ginger," she told me
one day, "some of us are cleaning the house of a woman
who has multiple sclerosis and cannot do it for herself."

Within six months Linda had begun dropping a lot
of weight. A local health agency called the Review to
find out why she no longer needed any medication for
her depression. Things were looking up for Linda.

At times I would go to her place. What fear I felt

when, on one of those visits, we heard loud footsteps coming up the stairs! *"Shhhh,"* she admonished. "It may be Jason, and he may be drunk." What a relief when it turned out to be their neighbor!

One afternoon Linda held out her hand to me and showed me an engagement ring. For reasons only God knows, I replied only that it was pretty. Linda invited me into her small kitchen that day to see the new sign that she had placed there: "As for me and my house, we will serve the Lord."

Finally she asked, "Ginger, aren't you going to ask me if I'm going to marry Jason?"

I responded, "You will tell me when you want me to know."

"Well, I am not." She seemed happy to say the words. "Jason drinks and smokes and sleeps around. I will never marry him."

A CALL IN THE NIGHT

More than a year passed. What progress Linda made! She seemed to be basking in her new life. Then one summer night the ringing of the telephone woke me from a sound sleep. As I reached for the phone I glanced at the glowing clock. This couldn't be good. No good news came at 11:30 p.m.

"Hello."

"Ginger, this is Linda." You need to come to my house quickly. I'm going to kill myself, and I need you to get here and take the girls."

Now I was awake. Dennis had awakened too.

91

"Wait, Linda; don't do anything. I'll be right there."

Knowing the area, Dennis had no intention of letting me go alone. We jumped into the car and drove over there together. Linda let us in.

"I CAN'T WAIT ANY LONGER TO DIE"

The old demon of fear had beaten Linda down. Afraid she would have to die for Jason, she could no longer sleep. Her life had become more and more intolerable as each night she kept expecting the death angel to strike her while she slept. Sleeplessness was taking its toll. We sat down with Linda. I opened my Bible to Psalm 4:8 and read to her: " 'I will both lie down in peace, and sleep; for You alone, O Lord, make me dwell in safety.' "

We helped her find a Christian radio station and encouraged her to keep the television off. I suggested that she open her curtains in the morning and let the sunshine in to give her a feeling of joy and energy. Finally she told us that all would be well. Later, into the wee morning hours, we had a hard time going to sleep.

Linda fell in love with Jesus. Her trust in Him developed as the days went by. Her language changed. She visited our church a couple of times. Her great wish was to see both of her daughters attending an Adventist school.

Again, a call came from Linda. This time it came at midday. "Ginger, you won't believe it. I'm getting married. He's a great man—he doesn't drink, smoke, or sleep around."

I'LL BE LOOKING FOR LINDA

I received her last call a few months later. Linda was married in a very small service. She was moving. Jason had broken her nose and battered her a bit as she and the girls had moved out. Yet she had excitement in her voice.

Some friendships are meant for only a season or two. I'll be looking for Linda on those streets of gold.

---

*The names of those in this chapter have been changed.

Chapter 12

"YOU DID *WHAT?*"

*"Now it happened one day that Elisha went
to Shunem, where there was a notable woman,
and she persuaded him to eat some food. So it was, as
often as he passed by, he would turn in there to eat some food.
"And she said to her husband, 'Look now, I know
that this is a holy man of God, who passes by us regularly.
"'Please, let us make a small upper room on the wall;
and let us put a bed for him there, and a table and
a chair and a lampstand; so it will be, whenever he
comes to us, he can turn in there' " (2 Kings 4:8-10).*

*"And the Syrians had gone out on raids, and had brought
back captive a young girl from the land of Israel. She waited
on Naaman's wife. Then she said to her mistress, 'If only
my master were with the prophet who is in Samaria!
For he would heal him of his leprosy' " (2 Kings 5:2, 3).*

*"Now an angel of the Lord spoke to Philip, saying,
'Arise and go toward the south along the road
which goes down from Jerusalem to Gaza.'
This is desert. So he arose and went" (Acts 8:26, 27).*

*"But a certain Samaritan, as he journeyed, came where
he was. And when he saw him, he had compassion.
So he went to him and bandaged his wounds, pouring on
oil and wine; and he set him on his own animal, brought
him to an inn, and took care of him" (Luke 10:33, 34).*

Perhaps you have found yourself wrestling with the same problems that I have faced so often. "Lord, how can I make a difference? I am only one, and there is so much need in this world. Answering Your call for service to others is far beyond me. I am not clever. I have no new ideas." These thoughts are only the beginning of a host of ways you and I excuse ourselves from being "God's servants."

Each excuse uses a key word: "I!"

Through the years I have learned one thing and learned it well. "I" can do nothing! "I" am sinful, and weak, and blind. "I" am a child! Jesus says it best: *"With [men and women] it is impossible, but not with God; for with God all things are possible" (Mark 10:27).* On my own, nothing but failure will be my lot. But when God takes over my life . . .

The human mind says either *You are not good enough* or *You don't need any help!* Paul says, *"But by the grace of God I am what I am, and His grace toward me was not in vain; but I labored more abundantly than they all, yet not I, but the grace of God which was with me" (1 Corinthians 15:10).*

Do you see the picture? Throughout the Bible we see men, women, and children living their ordinary lives under the direction of an extraordinary God. Does God require more of us today? As He has done throughout history, can God use each one of us in exactly the way He sees as best?

"I'M WILLING, LORD, BUT *WHAT CAN I POSSIBLY DO?*"
Susan★ had a passion to serve God. You could call it

a "burning desire." Only Susan had no plan. A week passed—nothing came to her mind. Two weeks passed—what could she do? "God, I won't give up. I'll pray every day until You bless me. I'll be on my knees begging You to use me. Until You show me some-thing—anything—that I can do, I won't lose hope!"

Into the third week Susan picked up the newspaper. She skimmed the pages, but they held little interest for her. Suddenly her eyes alighted on a strange assortment of want ads. *Want ads,* Susan said to herself. *I could write better ones than these.*

One in particular caught her eye: "Anyone inter-ested in facing the rising sun, call this number."

Well, I could do that. I could place a want ad in the news-paper. I want to give Bible studies. So, shortly afterward, Susan wrote her own ad: "Former SDAs interested in studying the Bible, call [Susan's phone number]."

"How I misjudged God's power," Susan told me a few months later. "Within the next few weeks I had 51 responses to that ad. Many wanted to know: 'What is an SDA?' When I told them that it stood for Seventh-day Adventist, these sincere men and women requested Bible studies anyway. One man responded by saying, 'I really don't want Bible studies, but could we date?'"

More than 30 studies resulted from that one short ad. Only eternity will reveal the complete story.

I'm one of the least—but I love God

Life had been hard for Barabara, a young mother living in a run-down apartment complex. She spent much of her time trying to make ends meet for herself and her children. How could she find time for soul winning?

"But I needed to let my neighbors know about God," Barabara told me that day. "One day I found the most wonderful sign—small, but to the point. On it were printed the words 'As for me and my house, we will serve the Lord.' I hung it on my front door immediately. Then my children and I talked about always living like 'God's children.'"

A few weeks later a stranger knocked on Barabara's door. "Excuse me—you don't know me, but I'm one of your upstairs neighbors. Every day my family and I see that sign on your door. We do not know Jesus. Would you tell us about Him?"

One sign, one family in the neighborhood, four baptisms.

But Barabara had only begun sharing God's love with others.

One cold morning she placed her great need of transportation before God. The day before, she had found a car; now she needed funds to purchase it. After calling a woman at her local bank and talking for a while, Barbara began to feel that everything was coming together.

"Do you want to sign up for the loan?" the woman finally asked.

"I believe so, but could you give me an hour or so to talk to my financial adviser?"

"Oh, you have a financial adviser?" The bank representative seemed a bit surprised.

"Oh, yes," Barabara replied enthusiastically. "I have to talk to my friend Jesus."

Silence hung for a moment on the other end of the line. Barabara began to wonder if the woman had hung up. "I don't know Jesus" was her unexpected reply. "Will you tell me about Him?"

It was a request Barabara eagerly honored.

"BUT I'M NOT DOROTHY!"

Sickness on the road—a dreaded occurrence to be avoided at all costs. *Note to self: Do not get sick on the road. When you travel, pay extra-close attention to the eight laws of health. The extra effort will bring great rewards!*

That's why I found myself walking around the hotel parking lot that cool but beautiful Sabbath afternoon. I had been invited to be one of the speakers at a women's retreat, and for the next hour we'd been given this wonderful gift of free time. I determined to make it count.

Once around. Twice around. *H'mmm . . . I think about six trips ought to do it.* I had nearly completed my third round when I looked to my left and saw a woman weeping. *Why would she be crying?* I asked myself, but no answer came. *She's surrounded by others; I'll just keep going.*

I looked the other way and picked up my pace. *She'll be gone by the next time I get around there,* I promised myself. She wasn't! *Is she crying out loud now, instead of quietly weeping?* I wondered.

Well, you can't take care of everybody, my common sense told me. I kept walking. The voice came swiftly: *"Dorothy Watts would have gone to her and hugged her!"*

But I'm not Dorothy Watts. I'm Ginger Church. She's surrounded by many friends, and I'm not going to just butt in. I walked on, my speed once again building—all the while assuring myself that my resolution to "mind my own business" was definitely the correct one.

My fifth trip around almost didn't happen. Perhaps so many trips around were a bit excessive. Of course, four would do the job. The battle in my head and heart raged on. *Stop and give her a hug. You know what Dorothy would do! Are you just going to turn your head and walk on by? What if you were in so much pain?*

The beautiful picture of Dorothy Watts, my friend and the women's retreat speaker the year before— touching, caring, ministering to those around her— would not leave me. I could not walk by again. So I promised God, "OK, if the crying woman is still there, I will go over and give her a hug. Now, *please,* help her not to be there!"

Joining the small group, I found myself wondering what to do next. Reaching out my arm to her, I spoke: "You look so sad; can I give you a hug?"

It was a toothache. The pain seemed unbearable. She accepted the hug, and I went in search of help—she needed a dentist.

Later that evening the young woman's mother came to me with a hug of gratitude. A dentist had been found—the infection had been serious. They had caught it just in time, and she would be OK.

"Ginger, I am a nurse," her mother shook her head. "I should have known the signs. I guess because it was my daughter, I just didn't pay enough attention. This was her first time ever to an event like this. She had enjoyed everything so much—I guess the devil wanted to keep her away. Thank you for caring enough to stop and help us."

"And thank You, God, for not giving up on me!"

"IS THIS THE *MESSAGE* OFFICE?"

Julie sat in her office, busily organizing the work to be done for two busy editors. *Working for* Message *and* Celebration *magazines sure gives me lots to do,* she mused. The shrill ringing of the telephone brought her back to the present.

"Hello, is this *Message?*" an irritated voice asked from the other end of the line.

"Yes, this is the *Message* office," Julie responded.

"Is *Message* a magazine?" the even more irritated voice quizzed. "Does this magazine talk about Jesus? It made my house a mess. It saved my life." She talked on, but Julie could not make out all that the woman said because of the tears/anger/great sorrow in her voice.

Julie asked the overwrought woman her name, and gave her the necessary information to call the nearest Adventist Book Center so she could purchase a subscription. Then Julie came into my office. "I got the most awful call just now. The woman was so agitated and rude. I'm sort of worried about her."

Julie and I discussed the call and prayed for the caller; yet we still worried about this distressed woman. I suggested that Julie call information in Pennsylvania to try to get her phone number. With only a city, a post office box, and a husband's name, we feared it would be impossible. But Julie's mission was successful. A few moments later a very shook-up Julie once again entered my office.

"Ginger, I called the woman. You know that part about the 'mess' and 'Christ in the magazine' and 'it saved my life'?"

"Yes."

"That woman had planned to commit suicide this morning. She and her husband had moved about six months ago, and she felt too alone and discouraged to go on. Yet this precious woman felt it would be best to clean up the mess her husband had left before she ended her life."

Julie could hardly contain herself.

"You know, Ginger, how the Review and Herald shreds the first few magazines that run through the press before it achieves the correct color—and then the shreds are sold as scrap? Her husband had received a large box of tools packed in these shreds. As this woman began cleaning, she thought she saw the word 'Christ' on a small scrap. She spent the rest of the morning trying to put together the masthead so that she could get a copy and find out what this magazine says about Christ before she died."

Julie arranged for a pastor to visit her new friend. This homesick daughter of God found friendship and hope. She fell in love with this Man named Jesus. Often Julie would call her, and they rejoiced together when this woman and her husband were baptized a few months later.

Be willing. Be alert. Be prepared. God will do the rest!

"BRENDA, YOU MADE ME *SO* SICK"

This could not be happening! How could I be sick? I'd been careful and not eaten too much; I'd drunk enough water, and taken my walk. During my prayer time I'd asked God to keep me safe and well, and now this—*2:30 in the morning, and I'm so sick I can't even focus my eyes. To make matters worse, I need to be on my way by 9:30, because I want to catch an earlier flight than the one I scheduled. With a three-hour drive to Omaha, Nebraska, I need to shake this terrible sickness.*

That Friday night and Sabbath had been wonderful. We'd enjoyed great music, Jesus had been near during the meetings, and on Saturday night I'd spent some time helping in the bookstore and telling everyone goodbye.

Now, in my great distress, I turned on the Christian radio station I had found on Sabbath morning, but I couldn't stand the noise. I reached for the remote and turned on the television. I couldn't focus my eyes. Desperate, I took a hot shower and a couple aspirin, and called the front desk to cancel my wake-up call. I always woke up by 7:30 or 8:00—I'd just have to give up on catching the earlier flight.

I woke up slowly and turned toward the clock by my bed. How I wished for a bit more time. The pain had subsided, but I still felt stiff and weak—this would be a hard day!

No! This couldn't be happening. How could it be 10:50? I not only felt dreadful, but now I would have to hurry just to catch my scheduled flight. But in the shape I was in, hurrying didn't seem to be an option.

The ringing of the phone jarred me into reality. Who could be calling at this time of morning? Everyone who knew my plans would assume that I'd already left. "Hello, this is Ginger."

"Oh, this is Brenda. I'm so glad I caught you. Can I come and talk to you for a few minutes?"

I suggested that she come in 10 minutes. What would it look like if she found me in bed at 11:00 a.m.? It took every bit of strength I had to shower and get dressed in that length of time. Exactly 10 minutes later I heard a light knock at my door. I opened it and invited Brenda in.

Brenda was small and lovely. Again, she apologized for intruding as I was getting ready to leave. In my weak state, I invited her to take a chair at the table where we could sit and talk. I asked her if she wanted to tell me a story.

"Oh, Ginger, you don't know how excited I am that you are still here. You see, my pastor's wife and I talked until 2:30 this morning about how to keep our children close to Jesus. Then we got on our knees by my bed and prayed that the Lord would not let you leave until I could talk to you."

Tears sprang from my eyes and rolled unchecked down my cheeks. "Oh, Brenda. You made me so sick!" Understanding washed over me. "Last night I went to bed safe in the knowledge that God would take care of me. At exactly 2:30 a.m. (I looked at the clock) I awoke—sick, with no idea why I should feel that way. You see, I had eaten very little last night so that I would have a good night's sleep."

"I'm so sorry! We just knew that I had to get to you."

"Tell me why, Brenda."

BRENDA'S STORY

"When I was a little girl in China, I was tricked into becoming a Seventh-day Adventist Christian."

My face must have shown wonder, because Brenda hurried on to explain.

"No, you see, I, like so many of the children, wanted to read English. I went to language school until I was 12. Then I had to go to work.

"But one of my friends found a school on Saturday that would teach children more about reading. This reading was done from the Bible. They taught us about health and about Jesus. I fell in love with Him. When the teacher asked how many wanted to be baptized and give their life to this Jesus, I gladly raised my hand.

"When my parents learned about this Jesus, they were very angry. They would tie me to a chair on Saturday morning to keep me from going to the Sabbath school, and beat me. I would not be swayed. Finally my father held up a butcher knife and told me he'd rather that I be dead than to worship this Jesus. My siblings begged for my life. My parents told me to gather my things—I would no longer be a part of their family.

"As I packed my few belongings, my mother warned me, 'Brenda, if you are going to do this, do not lose your bowl!'"

My face must have showed my lack of understanding.

"You see, Ginger, in China, a beggar uses a bowl to get money and to eat from. If you lose your bowl, you have nothing. My mother was telling me that if I lost this 'Jesus' I would have nothing, because I had already lost my family.

"God was good to me. A wonderful family took me in. I came to America, and now I have a wonderful family of my own. Yet, as I go to church, I often see children who are unhappy because they have been made to go to church. I hear parents talking about children who are angry over the standards of the church and how they have to force their children to attend church and other functions.

"That's why we were on our knees last night. You see, we were praying that you would go back to the Review and Herald and beg them to print a version of the book about the church's 27 fundamental beliefs for children ages 6-12. I want my children—and children everywhere—to love Jesus so much that they would be willing to die for Him. What if children everywhere worshipped God because they loved Him more than anything?"

ANSWERED PRAYER

Truly God kept me there in that hotel room. Together the two of us knelt by our chairs and pleaded with God for children everywhere, and that Brenda's dream would become a reality. I did go back and share her story with many at the Review—and with others at every possible opportunity. Brenda's dream became my passion: helping children everywhere understand that Jesus loved them enough to die for them—and that living for Him is our only safe option. We can trust Him, we can love Him; following Jesus is worth giving up everything we have.

★ Names in this chapter have been changed.

Chapter 13

SAVED FOR A REASON

*"Before I formed you in the womb I knew you;
before you were born I sanctified you; I ordained
you a prophet to the nations" (Jeremiah 1:5).*

Doug, our firstborn, came into this world laid-back like his father. Babies were easy. You feed them, change them, give them attention, and let them sleep. No problem. Some are like that.

Dony, our second son, could not have been more different. He turned over at three weeks, began walking the day he turned eight months. By his first birthday he had climbing out of his crib down to a science. It seemed there was nothing in the house that he couldn't conquer.

Often I asked Dennis how we would ever keep Dony alive until he reached adulthood. No matter how carefully we watched our "more active son," trouble, pain, and suffering seemed to hound him. From the scare of meningitis to getting his leg caught in bicycle spokes. The doctor assured us that Dony was surely a "miracle" when, at age 8, he accidentally ran through a glass door. Eighty-five stitches later we held him tight and knew that God must have a special plan for Dony to have kept him from even more extensive injury.

---

*"**Ordained.** Heb. *nathan,* 'to give,' here used in the sense 'to appoint.' A similar prenatal choice was made of John the Baptist (Luke 1:15). Jeremiah might have refused to comply with the divine call. All men are endowed at birth with certain possibilities, but it is their responsibility to develop these possibilities to the full. Likewise God has a plan for every life today. 'The specific place appointed us in life is determined by our capabilities' (Education, p. 267). We should discover what this place is and seek to carry out God's purpose and plan for us" (The Seventh-day Adventist Bible Commentary, vol. 4, p. 354).*

Day by day our boys grew. Through all these years I prayed for Doug's wife and Dony's wife. "Lord, keep them safe. Help them to have a heart for mission. Help each of the boys to know when they have found that special person You want them to spend their life with. Help Dennis and me to be supportive and in love with the girls who will become our "daughters."

Doug met his wife-to-be in driver's ed class when they were both in their sophomore year of academy. Seven more years would pass before they married, but I knew that God had answered my prayers and that we had been given an excellent blessing with this new daughter.

Dony dated, but could not find that special someone he wanted to spend his life with. "When, God?" I would ask. "When will Dony find his perfect wife? Have I not prayed hard enough? Will he remain single?" After he graduated from college, this fun-loving son returned home, and my prayers doubled. "God, will he be able to find her? Where is she? Have You made him to remain single? Surely not . . . ! A wife would give him so much joy. And Lord, he'd make a wonderful father."

It may be that you've also had your dreams dashed. The life that you had imagined for your children just doesn't seem to be the one they are choosing. Sharing my fears with Dennis didn't bring much relief. He would just smile and say, "Don't worry, honey. He'll be all right. He's happy and busy."

Why is it taking so long?

IS THAT ANY WAY TO ANSWER A MOTHER'S PRAYER?

He stood over me that day, silently waiting for me to look up. Busy at my weeding but noticing some unexpected shade, I glanced up and noticed him standing calmly there. Dony, our younger son, had graduated from college a couple of years before and accepted a job at the Review and Herald Publishing Association, where Dennis and I worked. We enjoyed his company and welcomed his energy into our lives.

Had I looked carefully, I would have noticed right away that today his usually smiling face held an unexpected seriousness. Engrossed in the enjoyment of spending the day outside and happy at the task of making our bit of heaven more beautiful, I managed a quick "Hi" and continued on with my work, waiting for his response while I worked. How beautiful our acre-plus of rocks, trees, and flower gardens!

"Mom, I need to talk to you," he began.

"Go ahead, Dony. You talk; I'll just keep on weeding while I listen."

"This is serious, Mom. I need to see your eyes. I need your full attention."

He had my attention. I moved to the steps and waited expectantly—for what, I did not know.

"Mom, you know that I have had America Online on my computer and how long it takes each time I try to connect. It became so frustrating that a few weeks ago I decided to discontinue it. As I was in the process, I saw these 'want ads.' Placing one didn't seem as though it would be too hard, so I decided to do it."

I didn't know whether to laugh or smile. *What was he telling me?*

"I just wrote something about a Christian male looking for the friendship of a Christian female." He laughed and continued on. "It didn't take long for the answers to start coming. Before long I was in a chat room with eight girls. They all wanted to know what kind of Christian I was. Then I moved out of the chat room. One, Mom, really has my attention."

What could I say? I had marveled at the laughter that had wafted from his room lately. *Could this be the reason?* I said nothing. *Where is he going with this story?*

"Her name is Michelle, and she wants to meet me. I told her that I thought it would be best if I flew to Arizona to meet her. I trust you and Dad. What do you think? Can I have your blessing?"

Time seemed to stop. "Be not unequally yoked" rushed to my mind. I almost bit my tongue to remain quiet. *God, help me! He's Your child. I gave him to You, God—we dedicated him to Your service. Please, give me wisdom.*

Finally I knew the answer. "Dony, if you are going to have a relationship with Michelle, I think it would be best if you met her. Let's go tell your dad."

They met in the Phoenix airport a few weeks later. "I knew she was the girl for me the first time I heard her voice," Dony told me later.

MICHELLE SPEAKS

"I guess I always knew I'd fall in love; I just didn't know how or when. God has a funny way of making things happen in His time, and when He has a plan, absolutely nothing can stand in His way. That is what I found in my love story.

"Our first contact came in July 1997. I had just purchased a computer and could hardly wait to get on the Internet to find lesson plans for my classroom. While learning my way around, I happened across a service on America Online (AOL) that allowed members to meet other members without the use of chat rooms. I thought to myself, *Now, meeting Christian men from around the country would be fun.*

"Clicking here and there, I discovered a list of Christian men who wanted to talk to Christian women, so I clicked on a few to just say 'Hi.' What happened next is something only God could have arranged.

"A few of the men wrote back, and one in particular caught my eye. He sounded sincere, not trying to impress me, just wanting a friendship. Quickly I decided

I wanted to get to know him better. Knowing we'd never meet, we talked freely, not trying to impress the other. In fact, we talked every day.

"We began to know a great deal about each other on the inside and grew curious about what the outside looked like. Cautiously we exchanged addresses and discussed exchanging photos. Then the worry began. *What if my hair is too short? What if I'm too fat?* Finally I decided that it didn't really matter. After all, we were never going to meet.

"Yet I grew anxious to see what 'Dony' looked like.

"The package he sent to me finally arrived. Before opening it, I asked Jesus to let me see Dony Church through His eyes. I knew that I liked this guy for what was on the inside, and the outside was unimportant.

"Days sped by; we enjoyed our e-mail chats more and more. And though I'd never dreamed it possible—with Dony in Maryland and me in Arizona—we began planning to meet. The word 'excited' doesn't begin to describe my anticipation; and, as you might imagine, also a little fear. I just had to keep in mind that God was truly in control.

THE NEXT BIG STEP

"The next big step for us was talking on the phone. We'd spent a lot of time on the Internet, but we had never heard each other's voice. The time had come.

"We were both nervous, and expected it to be a little awkward. We talked about it and decided to pray together the very first thing. God's plan had been perfect so far; why should we take over now?

"What great joy to hear Dony's voice after a month of written 'talking'! Words can hardly describe it. I knew something special had to be happening.

From virtual to the "real thing"

"Still, we were both eager to meet. So far all we'd been on were virtual dates. Our first date was mountain biking in Arizona. Dony enjoyed the awesomeness of the Sonoran Desert as I described to him the scenery, the animals, and, of course, the cacti.

"Then Dony treated me to a 'live' performance of *Cats* in Washington, D.C., followed by a tour of the D.C. Mall. Hours passed as we used our God-given imaginations to create 'dates' that would remain in our minds forever.

"Finally the big day came. I felt nervous—and excited! Everything had to be perfect.

"I arrived at the airport with an hour to spare. Oh, the agony! I wanted to meet him. I remember how I prayed as I waited for him to arrive.

"From the pictures he'd sent, I felt pretty confident that I'd recognize Dony right away. Finally I saw him. I can't say what went through my head at that moment. I just know I was overjoyed to see the man I had fallen in love with across the miles.

"Later Dony told me, 'Michelle, you stood there so still, almost frozen to the floor.'

"He walked up to me and gave me a hug. I hugged him back, but my feet were planted on the floor.

GOD WITH US

"We imagined our meeting being a bit awkward at first, but we were both happily surprised. As soon as we got to the car we prayed. It's funny how praying always brings peace to the most anxious spirit. I felt better then, reminded of who was in control.

"Dony's weekend in Tucson sped by in a heartbeat. We spent most of our time talking and just cherishing each other's company. We also discussed meeting again, this time in Maryland in October.

"Apart again, we found the Internet boring and began talking on the phone more and more. September dragged by. We talked about my graduating from college in December and not being settled in a career. We also talked about marriage, and we knew that even though we'd known each other only a very short while, we both wanted to be together for the rest of our lives.

"The big day for me to fly to Baltimore finally arrived. Maryland looked just as Dony had described it. I felt overwhelmed by the love and warmth of his family. I knew I wanted to come back.

"The day before my return home, Dony asked me to marry him. He said he'd prayed about it a lot. 'I know I want us to be together for the rest of our lives,' he assured me. 'And I know that God has brought us together too.'

"I had also spent much time in prayer and knew that my answer, as well as God's, would be 'Yes!'

THE BIG DAY ARRIVES

"We set the date for January 11 and began immediately to make plans—not easy across country. The most important thing we did was to meet with his pastor's wife online (where else?) for premarital counseling, and I began seriously studying Adventist beliefs.

"My dog, Muffin, and I moved to Maryland in December, and soon I moved into the apartment Dony had chosen for us. How quickly the time flew as I settled in and finalized our wedding plans. The Sabbath before our wedding, I joined Dony's church and became an Adventist.

"Then, suddenly, it was our wedding day. We'd often prayed that the only thing people would see that day would be God. We tried to keep it simple, yet create my dream wedding.

"Our wedding turned out just as I'd imagined it would be. After a 'winter wonderland' reception, we left the church in a beautiful horse-drawn carriage, the driver looking just right in his black tuxedo—Dony and I waving at friends and for pictures, and, then, having the opportunity to share a few private moments.

"Truly our day had the storybook ending I'd often dreamed of as a little girl. That awesome ride gave us a perfect ending to the wedding and a perfect beginning to our wonderful life.

"I never imagined that this story would be mine. But with God anything is possible—even a divinely appointed e-mail romance. Dony and I want God to be glorified through our relationship and our story. We owe it all to our Best Friend and wonderful Lord and Savior, Jesus Christ."

Chapter 14

MORE MIRACLES

"A man's heart plans his way, but the Lord directs his steps" (Proverbs 16:9).

What joy Dennis and I found watching Dony and Michelle establish their new home together. Truly they were kindred spirits and had a real zest for living. Michelle loved the storms this area brought—especially the snowstorms. A particularly snowy night might find them out in his four-wheel-drive pickup pulling unlucky drivers out of ditches.

Michelle found a good job teaching. The children loved her, and she made great efforts to make their learning experience for that year a memorable one.

At times Michelle would sit in our sunroom on a Sabbath afternoon and wonder out loud, "Why did God find me? With so many people living lives without His leading, why did He choose me to bless?"

I would reply, "Michelle, you were a seeker. You were searching for God, and He had been drawing you to Him all of your life."

ASKING GOD A NAGGING QUESTION

More than a year passed, and often I would think back to that day in the flower bed when Dony had first told me about Michelle. *Why, God,* I would wonder, *did You direct me to say "Yes"? What about not being "unequally yoked" together with unbelievers?*

The answer came unexpectedly one day as I sat quietly reading the story of Samson. Samson had made bad choices in marriage. That was it. Samson had married a girl that wanted nothing to do with God—not a seeker, but a woman who would do all in her power to turn his heart from God. Michelle, on the other hand, had been seeking God with all her heart.

"I'M BECOMING JUST LIKE YOU!"

Often I would tell the family of God's wonderful leading as I traveled, and we'd each share stories of His miracles in our lives. One Sabbath afternoon Michelle surprised me with "Ginger, I'm becoming just like you."

"And how's that, Michelle?" I asked. She had my attention.

"You know we got that big snowstorm a few days ago," she began. "I wanted so much to go out and play in it. I could almost feel a snowball in my hand and see the snowman I could create.

"Yet I also knew that I still had papers to grade and some lesson plans that needed to be finished. So I stayed at school and sat down at my desk and began working. A few minutes later I heard Christian music. It seemed to be coming from right outside my door. I couldn't help wondering. I had to get up and go see who could be playing that music. You just don't hear Christian music in the halls of a public school.

"As I walked through the door, I came face to face with one of the cleaning women."

"I knew it." She seemed excited as she spoke to me. "I knew that you were a Christian. I need someone to pray with me. Can we pray together right now?"

God's perfect timing? We both knew the answer. Michelle had met one of God's divine appointments that day.

GOD OF THE IMPOSSIBLE

May 26, 2004. Michelle's story begins: "My 'bad day' started the night before. I looked everywhere, but couldn't find the Roger Morneau book I wanted to read. Grudgingly I picked up a different one in the Morneau prayer series, even though that title was not the next in order. As I read the story about his copier, which ran with no ink in it for years, I yearned for that kind of experience with God

"The next day began kind of blah, then got worse. Our two children, Hannah and Ethan, were missing their daddy. I felt a bit alone and out of sorts without my husband, Dony; and I wondered if my mother-in-law, Ginger, who was here to help out with the kids, would rather be with her sister or back at camp meeting.

"That morning we tried to arrange a special supper with my aunt Kathy and uncle Paul, but they weren't sure they could come. While Ginger took her morning walk, I talked to some friends and invited them to join us for supper. They, in turn, invited other friends.

"In the end, everyone showed up at Jalapeños. With so many, our table was right out in the middle of the room. Aunt Kathy, who didn't know about the large-group thing and longed for quiet after a hard day's work, did not seem really excited about being part of a large crowd. She and I immediately shut each other out, and silence hung between us.

"Supper went on as planned. Everything was fine on the surface. Until my mother-in-law and I got back into the van. 'Didn't you tell your sister that more people would be coming?' I asked incredulously.

"'No,' she replied, 'I wasn't even sure that they would come. If they did, I thought perhaps I'd just sit at a different table so we could visit more easily.'

"We both tried to convince the other that our decision had been the right one. Finally my mother-in-law suggested that 'I shouldn't take things so personally,' and we settled into silence. There were no more words to be said.

"When we got home and were getting the kids out of the car, I heard the van go *ding, ding, ding,* and I thought, *What was that for?* (first prompting of the Holy Spirit), but I ignored it. The thought came to me that I should probably pull the van in a little more (second prompting of the Holy Spirit). Since I was going out later to have 'prayer time' with a friend, I decided to just leave it where it was and not close the garage door.

"I got Hannah out of her seat, and Ginger got Ethan

out of his. I closed the door on my side; then Ginger pulled hers shut. Suddenly, as we were all walking into the house, we heard a click. The van doors had all locked.

"Now, the doors locking wouldn't have been so bad, except I had left my purse in the van with my keys and the only spare key to the van (Dony's) in it. The house keys, the pickup keys, and my cell phone were also in my purse.

"I was beside myself. 'How could this have happened?' I snapped at Ginger.

"On the phone with Dony, I pleaded, 'Get me out of this mess. You've got to fix this!'

"Well, Dony, in another state at camp meeting, was minutes away from getting up to sell books at the evening sale. He suggested that I call OnStar, arrange for us to start a trial month, and then ask them to unlock our van.

"As we hung up the phone, the Holy Spirit spoke to me. 'Michelle, haven't you been learning about trusting God? When you feel anxious, you are not trusting!'

"'Well,' I snapped back, 'where have You been this whole day? It's not been one of my best!' Suddenly I was reminded that God doesn't promise that every day will be perfect—after all, we're living in the land of the enemy!

"'OK, Lord. I will trust You, but please get me out of this.'

"After getting Hannah ready for bed and putting Ethan to bed, I started looking, hopefully but unsuccessfully, for a spare key to the van. I already knew that one did not exist, but I could hope!

"All I found was the spare key to the pickup—actually, the key used to make spare keys. *Well, this key goes to a General Motors truck, and our van is also General Motors; I'll try it and see if it works.*

"So I went out to the garage and tried it in every door. Of course, nothing happened. I went to try it on the pickup, to make sure that it really was that key. Yes, it was, for sure, the spare to the pickup.

"Suddenly the story I had read the night before of Roger Morneau's copier flashed into my mind. So I whispered a prayer and boldly stood next to the van with the key in the lock. 'Lord,' I pleaded, 'if You can do that to his copier, You can open our van with this pickup key. You know that I have no way out of this and that we really can't afford to have a locksmith come or purchase and activate OnStar for a month. Besides, Lord, I really want to pray with April tonight. Without Your help we will have to wait for someone to come, and then it will be too late for our prayer time together!'

"Again I tried the driver's-side door . . . nothing! I tried the back . . . nothing. I tried the passenger door. Still nothing. I prayed again, 'Lord, I believe. I need You to help me with this. I won't give up.'

"I tried the driver's door again—this time the lights flashed. Hope—then fear of setting off the alarm. What would I do then? My keys were all locked inside. But I kept trying. Nothing!

"Then I heard God speaking to me: 'Michelle, you really need to have a clean heart before I can work any sort of miracle here. Go inside and tell Ginger you are sorry for the way you treated her.'

"'OK, Lord.'

"Asking for forgiveness was not hard. I didn't want my way—I wanted God's blessing on my life. The knot in my heart immediately let go, and I felt perfect peace—a miracle.

"Again I prayed, 'Lord, my heart is clean—it's all Yours. I need Your miracle.'

"I tried the driver's door. Nothing.

"'I'm not giving up until You bless me. I know You can.'

"On to the back door—nothing! Again I tried the passenger door, almost holding my breath. *Click!* My mouth fell open, and my heart began praising God. *He's worked a miracle for me!* I immediately ran inside to tell Ginger and Hannah the good news. We dropped to our knees in thanksgiving.

"What a praise session April and I had later that night. 'My God is able!'

"He who made heaven and earth can use my pickup truck key to open the van door."

HIS ANSWER IS BEYOND
YOUR IMAGINATION

Imagine the conversations we'll have on the earth made new.

Adam, how did it feel to wake up to a beautiful new wife? Did you enjoy naming all the animals? How could you stand seeing the Garden of Eden and yet not being able to enter it? I'm so sorry that you lost two sons—one murdered by his very own brother. Did you ever get over the feelings of despair and loneliness?

Eve, were you upset when you began to see signs of aging? You must have been so perfect and beautiful. Were you worried about your figure when you became pregnant for the first time? How did it feel to go from "clothed in light" to having to wear "real" clothes?

Abraham, were you afraid when God asked you to sell everything and go to a place He'd show you? What did it feel like to have the king take your wife? Did you have any hope of ever getting her back?

Sarah, it must have hurt to have no children and then watch another woman bear your husband a son. Did you hate her? Would you tell me about facing motherhood at such an advanced age? How did you have the guts to join the king's harem, knowing that you were married?

Moses, Miriam, Aaron, Hannah, Elkanah, Samuel, Elijah, Elisha, Gideon, David, Solomon, Jonathan, Rachel, Leah, Rahab, Naomi, Ruth, Joshua, Jacob, King Nebuchadnezzar, Bathsheba, Daniel, Isaiah, Jeremiah, Ezekiel, Haggai, Mary, Joseph, Dr. Luke, Peter, John the Baptist, John Mark, Dorcas, Mary, Martha, Lazarus, Stephen, the little servant girl, Philip, the Ethiopian eunuch—so many men and women.

The Bible tells us story after story of men, women, and children—written with facts, yet sounding like fiction. Each character brings instruction to guide our lives through a lifetime of living. Their stories are told with imagination and encouragement, cited as living examples so that we can go forward with confidence. We see excellent actions, despicable choices, and unswerving obedience. To face disaster, despair, and sadness with grace and joy is the goal. What a joyous conclusion when we find our place in the heavenly mansions!

As I write this, one more change has come into my life. No longer am I employed at the Review and Herald Publishing Association—a job I expected to hold in some way until the Lord came or, if time should last, I would retire into another change of lifestyle. It's been a difficult change—one I didn't understand. Yet through it all, I know God said to me, "Ginger, My grace is sufficient. Trust Me. Do not think of tomorrow. Smile, even when it seems things can't get worse."

The first day Dennis left for work and I stayed at home, sorrow almost overtook me. What had I done wrong? I know that my angel, who is always at my side, caused me to open my Bible, my *Message* version that I've been reading recently, and turn to the introduction to Joel and begin to read, "When disaster strikes, understanding of God is at risk. Unexpected illness or death, national catastrophe, social disruption, personal loss, plague or epidemic, devastation by flood or drought, turn men and women who haven't given God a thought in years into instant theologians. Rumors fly: 'God is absent' . . . 'God is angry' . . . 'God is playing favorites, and I'm not the favorite' . . . 'God is ineffectual' . . . 'God is holding a grudge from a long time ago, and now we're paying for it'. . .

"It is the task of the prophet to stand up at such moments of catastrophe and clarify who God is and how He acts. If the prophet is good—that is, accurate and true—the disaster becomes a lever for prying people's lives loose from their sins and setting them free for God. Joel is one of the good ones: He used a current event in Israel as a text to call his people to an immediate awareness that there wasn't a day that went by that they weren't dealing with God. We are always dealing with God."

I read the entire book of Joel. I kept on reading. As I began the introduction to Zephaniah, once again it stopped me right in my tracks:

"We humans keep looking for a religion that will give us access to God without having to bother with people. We want to go to God for comfort and inspiration when we're fed up with the men and women and children around us. We want God to give us an edge in the dog-eat-dog competition of daily life.

"This determination to get ourselves a religion that gives us an inside track with God but leaves us free to deal with people however we like is age-old. It is the sort of religion that has been promoted and marketed with both zeal and skill throughout human history. Business is always booming.

"It is the sort of religion that the biblical prophets are determined to root out. They are dead set against it."

I bowed my head and prayed. "O God, they speak of me. Please, Lord, make this seeming disaster a blessing. Use me in this new condition to bless others. Give me peace—even though I have no understanding. Use this experience to make me grow.

"And Lord, come soon. Take us home with You. Bring to Your beautiful home those we've loved, those we've stretched for, sacrificed for, laughed with, and cried over. Invite us all to join that sea of witnesses who can say—with the voice of experience—it was worth it all! I would have lived my life no other way!"

MY FRIEND, ASK GOD FOR A MIRACLE

Bid Him to still your quaking heart. Invite Him to enter your sinful, deceitful heart. Beg Him to embolden your trembling spirit to be willing to do all that you can. Let the Holy Spirit utter your prayers of eagerness and readiness to follow God's bidding. Surely your life will never be the same.

I know—I answered God's call to "go, and make a difference."

Questions You May Ask

"O Lord, You have searched me and known me.
You know my sitting down and my rising up; You understand
my thought afar off. You comprehend my path and my
lying down, and are acquainted with all my ways.
For there is not a word on my tongue, but behold,
O Lord, You know it altogether. You have hedged
me behind and before, and laid Your hand upon me.
Such knowledge is too wonderful for me; it is high,
I cannot attain it. Where can I go from Your Spirit?
Or where can I flee from Your presence?
If I ascend into heaven, You are there; if I make my bed in
hell, behold, You are there. If I take the wings of the morning,
and dwell in the uttermost parts of the sea, even there Your
hand shall lead me, and Your right hand shall hold me.
If I say, 'Surely the darkness shall fall on me,' even the
night shall be light about me; indeed, the darkness
shall not hide from You, but the night shines as the day;
the darkness and the light are both alike to You.
For You formed my inward parts; You have covered me
in my mother's womb. I will praise You, for I am
fearfully and wonderfully made; marvelous are
Your works, and that my soul knows very well.
My frame was not hidden from You, when I was made in
secret, and skillfully wrought in the lowest parts of the earth.

Your eyes saw my substance, being yet unformed.
And in Your book they all were written,
the days fashioned for me, when as yet there were
none of them. How precious also are Your thoughts
to me, O God! How great is the sum of them! If I should
count them, they would be more in number than the sand;
when I awake, I am still with You" (Psalm 139:1-18).

PRACTICAL ANSWERS TO QUESTIONS
I HAVE OFTEN BEEN ASKED:

1. Will God ask me to travel?

Are you willing to travel? Is your life placed completely into His hands? Could it be that you are holding back a part of yourself? One of the greatest parts of serving God is that He says to us: *"Therefore do not worry about tomorrow, for tomorrow will worry about its own things. Sufficient for the day is its own trouble"* (Matthew 6:34).

If God asks you to travel, He will give you the grace and the ability to do His bidding. If, like Jonah, you run from Him, He will find you. *"Trust in the Lord with all your heart, and lean not on your own understanding; in all your ways acknowledge Him, and He shall direct your paths"* (Proverbs 3:5, 6).

2. How can I find my talent?

If one or more of your talents are buried, dig them up, dust them off, and begin immediately to multiply them for the Lord. If you feel that God has made you "good for nothing," realize that He has a plan for your life. Spend time in prayer. Talk to others about areas in which you can become involved with your church, your neighborhood, your family, and in a host of other ways.

Think about the interests God has given you. Do you enjoy cooking? Are you a prayer warrior? Do you sing, sew, or speak? Are you interested in writing, walking, listening? Visit with your pastor, an elder in your church, or your class teacher.

Seek God's will for your life. He says, *"Ask, and it will be given to you; seek, and you will find; knock, and it will be opened to you. For everyone who asks receives, and he who seeks finds, and to him who knocks it will be opened"* (Matthew 7:7, 8). That's a promise! You can count on God to answer His promises.

3. How do I know if God is using me?

Let me answer that with three verses, found in 2 Kings 6:15-17, of one of my favorite Bible stories: *"And when the servant of the man of God arose early and went out, there was an army, surrounding the city with horses and chariots. And his servant said to him, 'Alas, my master! What shall we do?' So he [Elisha] answered, 'Do not fear, for those who are with us are more than those who are with them.' And Elisha prayed, and said, 'Lord, I pray, open his eyes that he may see.' Then the Lord opened the eyes of the young man, and he saw. And behold, the mountain was full of horses and chariots of fire all around Elisha."*

When healing went out from Jesus, He knew because of His closeness with the Father. What about you and me? Have we asked God to open our eyes and show us when and how He is using us? Are we so closely attuned to our Lord that we are able to recognize the miracles that He performs for and through us? Are you more apt to use the words "I was lucky" or "I was blessed"?

4. How can I remember all that God has done for me?

The Bible tells us to speak of the things that God has done for us. In Bible times families built altars to the Lord. Those sacrifices were to bring remembrance to their minds.

Before we can remember the great things God has done for us, we must recognize them and in humble grace thank God for His wondrous works in our behalf. Make it a priority to talk of God's goodness to you, your family, and those you care about in your worship, at church, when you're riding, at work, and at play—in other words, whenever the opportunity arises.

5. I just want to give up; I'm so sad and alone. Can you help me?

God can help you. Even in our darkest hour He is with us. Ask Him to give you joy. (Remember, His blessings to Job were more than he had lost.) Ask God for a friend—just the one you need most. God loves to give good gifts to His children. Look for others who walk the same path you do. If you are sad because of health, remember all the times you enjoyed good health, and your healing will be increased.

If you've lost a spouse, a child, or a friend through death—even for reasons you do not know or cannot change—give your sorrow to Jesus and feel the warmth of His love.

Most of all, reach out to others. Spend time in prayer and Bible study. Psalm 73:28 says, *"But it is good for me to draw near to God; I have put my trust in the Lord God, that I may declare all Your works."* James 4:8-10 says it again: *"Draw near to God and He will draw near to you. . . . Humble yourselves in the sight of the Lord, and He will lift you up."*

6. How can I get my parent/spouse/grown children to start doing something or to do more?

God loves a cheerful giver, and I think that also goes for giving of ourselves to Him. The best way to lead others is by example. Are they seeing joy in your service? Are they seeing you serve? You can invite them to join you. You can help them develop their talents. You cannot speak for them. If you push them, you will probably drive them away from, not toward, service.

Yet, just as God has given us the power to choose whether or not we will love Him and serve Him, our family members will each make their own decisions. We cannot demand that they find joy in serving God. God draws us through His love. Can we do less?

7. Did you ever become discouraged?

The devil runs around Planet Earth seeking whom he can devour/discourage/disrupt. We live in the land of the enemy. Yes, I have walked through valleys and run on high hills—God has always walked with me or carried me. The most important question we can ask is not "Have we been discouraged?" but "What did we do with our discouragement?" In the end, did we use it for God's glory? Did we bless others from what we learned while in our valleys?

8. How do you accept thanks and compliments?

I once read a piece about Corrie ten Boom that gave me the answer to this question for myself. When asked this question, she responded, "I just gather up the compliments like a bouquet of flowers. Each evening I place them in a lovely vase and give them to Jesus, to whom they really belong."

A "Thank you" when complimented is very acceptable. "I'm glad you enjoyed it." "To God be the glory." "Thanks!" Anything except "It was nothing." Everything we do for God is something and should be acknowledged as such.

9. What if no one comes to an event at which I am speaking?

Sometimes we will speak to many and at other times to just a few. Jesus spoke to crowds (some who wanted to stone Him) and at other times to just one in the night or at the well. I do not worry about the number of people. My only thought is to bless those whom God loves and died for. God would have died if I had been the only sinner. If He sends me to speak to one, I'll speak with all my heart and rejoice in His service.

10. Who has helped you the most?

We do not live in a vacuum. There have been so many people along the way who have given me a hand. I am very grateful for Christian parents, encouraging siblings, and awesome children (and their families). I have also received encouragement from many of our church leaders and have learned from them in a host of ways.

Yet, throughout the past 38 years, Dennis has been my rock, my greatest encourager and supporter. He has always been there for me, as I have tried to do for him. His creative ideas and solid suggestions have helped me to develop and grow. I thank God daily for the love of this good man and know that his reward will be great in heaven.

HINTS FOR HAPPY HOMECOMINGS

Going home—it's the icing on the cake. Just the mention of it quickens one's heart and brings a smile. Yet often the simple act of returning causes a host of problems.

"Why isn't the house the way I left it a week ago?"

"Why didn't you call me more often?"

"Did you miss me? It doesn't exactly seem like it. Where is your excitement now that I'm here?"

"You did what?" "You ate *what?* Surely not at McDonald's (Burger King/Taco Bell/etc.)?"

"You didn't even *touch* my casserole—I worked so hard on it, even though I didn't have the time."

"Honey, I've learned some great things! We've got to change our lives!" These bits of dialogue, and many more like them, come only from the lips of the one returning.

Those left behind respond over the next few days with such things as: "Why are you so uptight? I should never have let you go!"

"I'm happy with our life the way it is!" "You bought what?" "Why are you always complaining about what I do?"

Having made some of these very errors myself, I

want to share a few of the things that I and others have learned about happy homecomings. In other words, tried-and-true suggestions for making the most of your time apart. Helpful hints for coming back together as one. Beating that spirit of "You did what?" or "Why didn't you?"

Spending time apart and then coming back together gives couples, parents, children, even friends, extra chances to grow and appreciate those relationships that can become humdrum to us unless they are treated with our utmost appreciation and attention.

Whenever you find yourself away from home, spend some time thinking about your homecoming. Here is an easy outline that may be of some help to you.

1. Pay attention to the children. Time passes differently for little people. They often sorely miss a loved one who is away. Make it your habit to get down at eye level with the little people in your life when you return—even when you've only been gone a few hours. Now—hug them and listen. Give them at least five minutes of serious listening.

"Guess what I did, Mommy [Daddy]! I went to church yesterday in my dirty dress/my hair looked funny/I didn't brush my teeth." No matter. Now is not the time to find fault. Some may have skipped church altogether. The secret is that you are glad to be home and back with them. Fussing and finding fault will not convey that message.

When your little one tells you that they ate out every meal or ate other than what you left, compliment them for their creativity and be glad they didn't go hungry.

Being the ones left behind can be lonely and hard work; on the other hand, it gives them the opportunity to "get out of the box" and try some new things they always wanted to do.

If those you have left behind did "good" in your absence, praise God and them! On the other hand, if they had a very hard time—you have work to do! None of us knows how long we have on this earth. It should be the duty of every parent, grandparent, husband, and wife to make sure that their beloved family members are able to take care of themselves, if for any reason you did not return.

A mother told me of coming home to find a large banner hanging in the kitchen. On it in very large letters were the words WE LOVE YOU! Suddenly tears of joy sprang unbidden down her cheeks. Seeing the reaction from his mother, the 7- and 9-year-olds rushed over to her.

"What's the matter, Mom?"

"It's that sign!" she said, pointing.

"Oh, yeah; we made that for Daddy." They chimed in together. "He was having such a hard time."

2. Give quality time to the adult(s) you left at home. Now is the time to listen—spend at least five minutes concentrating on what they did that they are eager to talk about and share with you. Make this a time of joy and appreciation. Laughter is good medicine. Enjoy the ones you love. If there are things that need to be discussed, hold them for later—much later.

Perhaps the place you left with pride for its cleanliness is now in a shambles—bite your tongue. You can clean it again. If the food you prepared still sits cold and hard in the freezer, rejoice—it will save you some cooking time later on.

Think of the glorious homecoming when Jesus returns! How do you want Him to greet you?

Get in touch with those at home while you are away. Give them a number where you can be reached. Questions often arise; they may have planned a surprise for your return. Remember the golden rule and keep the ones at home informed of your whereabouts.

3. Now it's your time. A funny thing happens after you have taken the time to love and listen to those who have stayed at home. Suddenly they look at you and ask, "How did your trip go?" You have five minutes! Don't overpower them with what you did or what you have learned. Over the next few weeks and months everyone will share, bit by bit, other things that are of any importance to them.

4. If you are the one who has been gone, you will probably be tired. Perhaps you have given much of yourself to others. Expect a period of letdown. You may have had only yourself to think about; now you are once again responsible for others. Do all that is within your power to spend some extra time with God and give yourself plenty of time for rest and renewal. Arrange some time for exercise and eat some of your favorite foods.

5. Add a hint or two of your own. Our families are

a bit of heaven here on earth. They should be full of joy and gladness. Don't let your guard down, but be vigilant always to make your earthly home a taste of the earth made new.

RESOURCES

The Adventist Home
Christ's Object Lessons
The Seventh-day Adventist Bible Commentary
The Voice in Speech and Song